Praise for Touched by a Miracle

This book opens the doorway to miracles by showing us real examples of what's possible with the skillful use of EFT. JoAnn SkyWatcher is both a master practitioner and a great storyteller.

Paul Zelizer, EFT Practitioner and Success Coach

I thought this was a very warm, personal, and thoroughly enjoyable book. I hadn't thought of tapping as creating miracles, but as I read JoAnn's heart-warming, back-to-back stories, the results do seem miraculous. What is so remarkable about tapping is that we can create our own miracles every day. *Touched by a Miracle* is a treasure.

Lindsay Kenny, EFT Master

JoAnn has penned an absolutely fabulous book on how to do the ART of EFT, written in plain English. It will take your practice to the next level.

Eric B. Robins, MD
EFT Advisory Board Member
Co-author, Your Hands Can Heal You

Touched by a Miracle will give tremendous hope and relief to so many. Kudos to JoAnn for putting into words the healing that takes effect through EFT. This book is alive with personal stories that everyone can identify with while teaching us how we can transform our lives in an instant. This is exactly what the world is waiting for!

Jewels Johnson, Creator, Law of Attraction Radio Network

This delightful collection of stories will inspire you to believe that miracles are possible. In a simple, direct style, *Touched by a Miracle* speaks to the wonderful possibilities inherent in EFT, in our ability to heal ourselves and heal the world.

Pamela Bruner, EFT Expert
Author, EFT and Beyond

Being an EFT Practitioner and Trainer, I am constantly amazed at the effectiveness and power of this humble little tool called Emotional Freedom Techniques.

Touched by a Miracle inspires and educates readers on the use of EFT in people's lives. JoAnn does a beautiful job of weaving stories, accounts, and cases from people of all walks of life who have been touched and transformed by this energy psychology technique.

I highly recommend *Touched by a Miracle*, which speaks both to tapping newcomers as well as seasoned practitioners. If you're new to EFT and want to learn more, pick up this book. And if you've been tapping for some time and want an extra dose of inspiration, this book is a must-read.

AnaMaria Herrera
EFT Practitioner and Trainer
www.SolutionFocusedEFT.com

If you've ever thought about trying EFT, or wondered if it would work for you, then *Touched by a Miracle* is for you! Reading the inspirational experiences of JoAnn's many clients will give you the confidence to take action and give it a try. She has an intuitive gift for getting to the core issues for her clients and bringing them to light. Truly a miracle!

JoAnn includes charts, processes, and tools to get you started in using EFT. Her calm and easy manner of being present with you comes through in each story. You will feel yourself being drawn into the process, almost as if you are there with JoAnn and her client. You may find you want to tap along!

Paula Tarrant
Certified Spiritual Life Coach and Transformation Expert
www.InspiredWomenWork.com

Great reading for anyone who wants a simple way to feel better now! I'll be sharing this book with my family and friends.

Eleanore Duyndam, Founder of EFT Radio Online

JoAnn's book is a graceful journey through the art of sharing how to do EFT, combined with vignettes of the beautiful healing many have gained through her skill. Storytelling is an ancient art that has been used for centuries as a playful way to share knowledge. JoAnn does this superbly. Yet the marvel is that her examples are of real people whose lives she has dramatically improved. *Touched by a Miracle* makes for a life affirming read.

Sejual Shah, Stress Resolution Specialist
www.HealthyinMind.com

JoAnn Skywatcher enriches us all with these clear, precise and profound examples of the effect of using the simple yet elegant tool of EFT in reclaiming our birthright of self-empowerment.

Angela Treat Lyon
the Live Artfully Coach
www.AngelaTreatLyon.com

I appreciate the candor, compassion and warmth that radiates from these pages. It is obvious that you are a passionate practitioner who creates both safety and the space for miracles to happen. Thank you for communicating so clearly your compassion and heartfelt joy. Reading your words strengthens my trust that miracles are alive in our world — and for that I am truly grateful.

Jade Barbee, www.EFTfree.net

This book will give you a very good idea of exactly what EFT can do for you and others. With a little familiarity with the technique, it soon becomes obvious why EFT is so effective. This book will give you an opportunity to see what it can do even if you haven't had the chance to experience the real thing yet. I highly recommend you check this out.

Reverend Tanya Wyldflower

JoAnn brilliantly takes us on a journey that introduces the healing modality of EFT, one that literally "taps" into the wisdom designed into the miraculous capacity of our body to heal itself.

Belvie Rooks, Growing Global a Heart

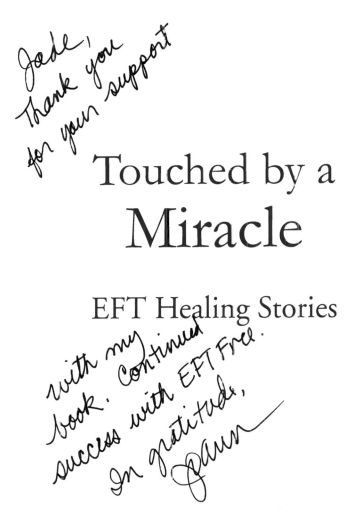

Jade,
Thank you
for your support

Touched by a
Miracle

EFT Healing Stories

with my
book. Continued
success with EFT Free.
In gratitude,
JoAnn

JoAnn SkyWatcher

Rock
Creek
Press

Published by
Rock Creek Press
PO Box 789, Ukiah, CA 95482 USA
www.rockcreekpress.com

Notice: Nothing in this book should be construed as a promise of
benefits or a guarantee of results to be achieved. The author and
publisher disclaim any liability incurred directly or indirectly as a
result of the use or application of any of the contents of this book.

Disclaimer: While EFT has produced remarkable results, it must be
still considered an experimental technology. By moving forward with
this instructional manual, you agree to take complete responsibility
for your use of EFT and for your emotional and physical well-being.
Neither JoAnn SkyWatcher or Rock Creek Press can be held liable for
how you choose to use these methods. If you feel in any way reluctant
to use these methods for yourself or others, please do not. Instead,
consult a qualified professional.

Book design and layout: Steve Ryals, Rock Creek Press
Cover design: Steve Ryals, Rock Creek Press
Editing: Steve Ryals, Rock Creek Press
Cover Photo: JoAnn SkyWatcher (www.joann-skywatcher.
artistwebsites.com)

ISBN 978-1-933906-43-0

10 9 8 7 6 5 4 3 2

Acknowledgements

First and foremost, I want to thank my beloved husband, Steve Ryals, for encouraging me to write, even though I didn't believe that I could. I would also like to thank you for the fantastic job you did on editing this material. Not only that, you did the typesetting and layout – it's beautiful! I so appreciate your attention to detail. I'm also grateful for your gentle encouragement and the way you held me through this process.

Kristin Frith, thank you for inviting me to the "Yes" Conference in 2003. It was at that conference that I was first introduced to EFT.

Thank you, Dr. Mercola, for including articles about the power of EFT in your newsletter. Your articles kept steering me towards Gary Craig's web site.

If Gary Craig had not been willing to put out so much information about EFT for free, I probably wouldn't have immersed myself in studying this valuable tool. Gary, I will be forever grateful.

I want to thank my son, Calvin Turnwall, for saying early on, "Mom, I think you are on to something with EFT." I needed lots of encouragement when I first got started.

My EFT friend, Paul Zelizer, repeatedly talked about the importance of social networking. His encouragement helped me embrace Twitter. Thank you, Paul!

I also appreciate the support of EFT Radio visionary, Eleanore Duyndam, for calling me all the way from New Zealand and encouraging me to continue to show up big in the world.

I especially want to thank all of my friends, relatives and even strangers who allowed me to practice with them.

Finally, a big shout out to Barbara Ryals, Gail Johnson, Tanya Wyldflower, Quana Ryals and Paula Tarrant for your meticulous eyes and generous hearts. You all helped make this a better book. Thank you!

Contents

Appendix

Introduction

Touched by a Miracle is a collection of healing stories that happened to me as well as to family, friends and clients I have worked with over the years. From my experience, I have come to believe that re-solving "issues" with our life situation could be called grace or even a miracle. At the very least, it's a wonderful thing.

The purpose of sharing these stories with you is multi-layered. One of my passions is to inspire you to consider the possibility of using Emotional Freedom Techniques (EFT) in your own life. If you're already an EFT Practitioner, I believe these stories may give you new insights into your own work. If you're a coach or counselor, these anecdotes may encourage you to incorporate EFT as a helpful tool. Another passion is to foster hope. No matter how dire your situation may appear, there is always hope.

Before going any further, I want us to be on the same page (tongue firmly in cheek) about what I mean when I use the word "miracle." I like yourdictionary.com's second definition, "A remarkable event or thing; marvel." For example, if you were suffering from an in-tractable migraine, you'd likely consider fast and lasting relief to be nothing short of a miracle.

Some people poo-poo the idea of miracles, that it's too Pollyanish. If you are able to consider the possibility of miracles, my belief is that you will experience them in your life, especially compared to the person who says something like, "No way in hell," or "I don't believe in miracles, that is just bulls**t." If you are open to the possibility of miracles happening, I believe that puts you into the Miracle Zone. Do you believe that you are worthy of miracles? Would like to see more miracles in your life? If so, there are concrete steps you can take today (see "How to be in the Miracle Zone" on page 162).

I believe that each of us has the power to heal ourselves. Of course, there are times when we may have to reach outside of ourselves to find help, but ultimately it is us (or, more precisely, the Power within) that does the healing. Actually, I don't think it much matters what you believe in terms of Who or What heals you, just that you believe in the possibility of healing itself.

I have explored the healing arts all of my adult life. In 1971, I received my teaching credential in Physical Education from Cal Poly at San Luis Obispo, California. In the early 70s, I found myself fascinated with subjects as diverse as progressive relaxation, the golden healing light, visualization, self-hypnosis, and yoga. Incorporating what I had learned, I taught classes mostly to adult women for seven years, including Stress Reduction, Physical Fitness for Women, Exercise for Pregnant Women and Physical Fitness for Senior Citizens.

In 1974, during the birth of Calvin, my first child, I experienced a profound shift in consciousness. When I first looked into my new baby's eyes, I saw a divine being gazing calmly back at me! It changed my life to see how we come into this world as God-Goddess. I realized that all of us are Divine sparks. Knowing who I really am, and who everyone else really is, makes a huge difference in healing and creating miracles. When I resonate with the vibration of this non-dual awareness, I am often able to achieve incredible results. Every time I presence this energy, I feel like a homing device to which others can attune.

For example, a friend I have known since I moved to Mendocino County in 1971 tells a story that happened over 30 years ago. One day, as "Nick" recounts the episode, he had arranged to come over for a visit. It turns out that he wasn't feeling well, and the walk to my house seemed as though it took hours instead of the usual 15-20 minutes. When he finally arrived, Nick was clearly in great distress. He described doubling over from the severe pain in his lower abdomen.

I urged him to lie down, and I gently placed my hands on his stomach. I asked him to join me in imagining "Golden Healing Light" surrounding and penetrating this painful area. Exhausted after our healing session, Nick slept as best he could in a tipi that stood in the garden. He later told me that he had screamed with pain during the night.

The next day Nick went to the emergency room at our local hospital, and was immediately operated on. After the operation, the doctor told him that he was very lucky to be alive. His appendix had burst, but there was something that the doctor had never seen in the thousands of appendectomies he had performed. The doctor said that part of Nick's peritoneum had somehow become wrapped around his appendix, sequestering enough of the toxic brew of his burst appendix from spilling into his abdomen, thereby saving his life.

Nick finished his story by sharing that he believed it must have been the healing work I had done with him the night before that had saved him. When I was working with Nick, I didn't even know he was having a problem with his appendix. I was simply using the "Golden Healing Light" and resonating love.

* * * *

Later in the 70s, I became a Universal Life Minister. Ever since, I have seen myself as a spiritual healer, even though I haven't been interested in leading a congregation. Over the years, I have performed a marriage ceremony for several couples, truly a highlight of being a minister.

In the 80s, I first began studying the teachings of Ernest Holmes, eventually completing the four-year Religious Science training to become a licensed Practitioner (now known as a Spiritual Coach). For years I headed the healing ministry at our center in Ukiah. It was during this period that I learned the power of affirmative prayer and spiritual alignment.

Around that same time, I began to appreciate the power of the breath and soon became a re-birther. As a re-birther, I guided people to re-live traumatic experiences as far back as birth or even conception, focusing on the breath while we cleared those traumas.

Also during the 80s, I wrote a newspaper column about affirmations called "Minders." In that column, I told short stories about people successfully using affirmations to positively affect their lives. I also included a short affirmation that I had written out in calligraphy so that people could cut it out of the newspaper and put it where they could be repeatedly reminded of it.

I became very curious about why affirmations didn't always work. I really didn't know what to do when people said their affirmations faithfully and yet nothing happened. If I had known about Emotional Freedom Techniques (EFT) in the 80s, I would have been able to help them. (Oh well, Gary Craig didn't develop EFT until the mid-90s.) Now I know what to do when people encounter resistance to their affirmations.

* * * *

EFT is an incredible tool that Gary Craig first introduced back in the mid-90s. If it weren't for Gary Craig, and all of the time and money that he has put into promoting EFT, I never would've had the opportunity to become aware of EFT's power.

My first encounter with EFT was in 2003. At that time, I was still teaching high school. I had taken a group of students to a health fair, and had the opportunity to go to an EFT presentation. You might be surprised to learn that my initial response was not positive. There were three basic issues that I had a problem with:

- What I interpreted as negative wording in the first part of the setup phrase. For example: "Even though my shoulder *hurts* ... ." I didn't want to say something I considered to be negative (owning the truth that I felt pain in my shoulder), thinking that it would somehow contribute to making the pain worse.
- How weird EFT looked to me. Especially, the 9 Gamut Procedure, where people were rolling their eyes around (which helps balance the right and left hemispheres of the brain).
- The enthusiasm that the instructor had about EFT, including her strong belief that it could work on anything.

I guess I just wasn't ready to embrace EFT at that time, though I never forgot about it. When I read articles on the Internet by Dr. Mercola, he often talked about a miracle cure for getting rid of a migraine headache. When I clicked on the link it would be to an article about EFT. I kept being surprised to see references to EFT's power. It took me two years of seeing similar references before I signed up to receive Gary Craig's (now defunct) newsletter.

As though a switch had been thrown, I jumped head-over-heals into the world of EFT. I downloaded and studied the free EFT manual Gary Craig made available, then started researching the newsletter archives and using their search engine to look up different issues.

I soon bought a set of Gary Craig's EFT DVDs. The information spoke loud and clear. I could see the often astonishing results on video. Though EFT still looked a little weird, I started tapping along with the videos and repeating as best I could the words Gary Craig used. Since I was having a problem with my short-term memory because of Lyme disease, I found it rather frustrating at first, but I persisted.

I began spending a lot of time watching EFT videos, taking notes and reading case studies, becoming a devout EFT student in the process. I bought even more of Gary's DVDs. On fire with wanting to learn everything I could about EFT, as soon as I came home from teaching I hopped on the computer and studied. I was thrilled to be able to learn almost for free while living in the middle of nowhere, off-the-grid.

After studying on my own for nearly a year, I began reaching out to my friends and family, trying EFT with many people on a wide variety of issues. For example, I might say to someone who was experiencing a headache, "I've been learning this weird-looking technique called EFT that might help your headache go away. It's a little bit like acupuncture but you don't need needles. EFT is all about releasing stuck emotional energy and returning to a smooth, harmonious flow. Do you want to see if we can make this headache go away?"

I often felt frustrated trying to explain EFT. Some people would look at me as though I was speaking a foreign language, while others were willing to give it a try. For the ones who were willing, in almost every single instance they felt better. In a number of cases the improvement felt like a miracle both to myself and the person who experienced it. The more I practiced EFT with people, the more excited I got. I guess you might say I became obsessed with it. Though I tried to tone it down, I wasn't very successful hiding my enthusiasm. The good part was that my confidence grew in leaps and bounds, because I had so much success with EFT.

You may choose to get really excited about EFT and become an practitioner – yay! If I could learn how to use it, it's totally possible that you can as well. I didn't start learning EFT until I was in my late 50s. I had a lot of uncertainty about whether I could learn how to use these powerful techniques, especially given my own issues with Lyme disease and my memory. Even though it seemed like a stretch, I used EFT to tap away my doubts and fears. So, if you want to do something that seems like a big stretch, I want you to know that you can do it. I trust that my story gives you hope to fulfill your dreams.

At some point in the process, you may decide to find a skilled EFT practitioner. If you do, I'd love to have you schedule an appointment with me. You can reach me at joann@wayhealthy.us, or call 707 462 2501. If I'm not available, some of the places you can look online to find EFT practitioners include:

- www.tappinginternational.com
- www.mttpronetwork.com

- http://nationalallianceforemotionalhealth.com
- www. aamet.org
- www.eft-therapy.com/eft-network/index.php
- www.tappingcentral.com/EFTPR/PractitionerList.htm
- www.eftfree.net

Like myself, the majority of EFT practitioners work mostly by phone, so you don't have to leave home to get help. I can personally attest to how effective phone sessions can be. If you prefer to work in person, you can often find someone in your area with whom you can have a face-to-face session.

Our thoughts are powerful. I use EFT to help people realign with their Essence. I see dis-ease (stress) happening when we get out of balance. I am able to help people release trauma as well as programming, beliefs and stories that no longer serve, and then come back into alignment and balance. This is my own individual way of doing EFT. I find the combination of using EFT with spiritual awareness to be incredibly potent.

The encouragement of my beloved husband, along with lots (and lots!) of tapping (to get rid of my old stories about not being able to write) has made this book possible. I do hope that you enjoy these empowering stories.

1

Releasing Pain:
Migraine Vanishes in 10 Minutes

EFT offers great healing benefits.
- Deepak Chopra, MD

During a class in which I was participating, "Laura" complained that she was having a hard time thinking because she had a migraine headache. During the break I asked her about it.

She described the pain as going from the side of her neck to behind her right eye. I asked if she had any idea what caused it. She said that she had missed her hair appointment, and she didn't like that. She also said she didn't like having a migraine. I asked what the intensity of the pain was, and she replied that it felt like a 9 out of 10.

We didn't have much time before class resumed, so I showed her how to tap on her karate chop point (see Tapping Charts on page 165) while repeating after me: Even though …

- I have a hard time thinking because my migraine headache really hurts, I deeply and completely love and accept myself.

- I missed my hair appointment and I didn't like that …
- This migraine headache hurts like hell …

I had her begin by tapping on the top of her head with both hands, saying, "Releasing this migraine headache." As I directed her to tap on the EFT points, I noticed that her inner eyebrow point seemed to be a "hot" one and had her give it some extra time. I could see her face relax as she repeatedly tapped that point. I also worked to get her to laugh, and make funny noises with her breathing to help shift the energy.

After she finished the first round of tapping, I asked her to close her eyes and notice how she felt. She said that she felt much better, and that the pain had gone down to an intensity level of 4. I then asked if any other information had come in, and she said that she had been worrying about money problems.

So, for the second round I instructed her to tap on her karate chop point and say: Even though …

- I still have a migraine headache …
- Even though I am worrying about money problems …
- Even though I am worrying about money so much that it has made my head hurt …

Then I had her tap on the top of her head and repeat, "Remaining migraine headache pain." Then, as she tapped the other points, I had her alternate the reminder phrases "migraine headache" and "money problems."

After finishing the second round, just before class resumed, she exclaimed, "The pain is gone!"

2

EFT Quickly Eliminates Painful Hornet Sting

EFT is a simple, powerful process that can profoundly influence gene activity, health and behavior.
~ Bruce Lipton, PhD

I was in a hurry to get to town for an appointment. As I reached into my country mailbox, I saw a hornet in the back, which is not unusual. The moment I picked up the mail I felt an "electric" shock on the side of my hand. One of those damn hornets had the unmitigated gall to sting me!

On a deadline to get to town, I needed to keep moving. I usually use essential oils for insect bites, but that day I had forgotten to carry them with me. Though my hand now throbbed with pain, I had to keep driving on our twisty country road. In that moment I thought of doing EFT! Because I had to pay attention to the road, it wasn't safe to use both hands and tap on my karate chop point. However, I did manage to drive with one hand on the steering wheel while rubbing the tender spot on my chest.

The tender spot is a couple of inches below the collar bone (see Tapping Chart on page 165). Some people prefer using the tender spot instead of the karate chop point, and others only use the karate chop point on the side of the hand because it is easier to find than the tender spot (also called the sore spot). My setup phrases included: Even though …

- I got stung by a damn hornet, and it hurts like hell, I deeply and completely love and accept myself.
- I hate it that I got stung by a damn hornet …
- There is a feeling like an electric shock on the side of my hand …

Then I tapped each EFT point, repeating my reminder phrase, *damn hornet sting* (sometimes I said *damn* with emphasis and sometimes I didn't say it at all). As soon as I tapped on my eyebrow point and the side of the eye point, I could feel the sting's painful intensity lessening. By the time I completed one round of tapping, I barely noticed the pain.

Like Gary Craig says, try EFT on everything. By the way, when I got to town about 20 minutes later, I couldn't tell exactly where the hornet had stung me. No red spot, no swelling, nothing at all except a quickly fading memory (and this story).

3

Excising Weight Loss Excuses

FOOD IS AN IMPORTANT PART OF A BALANCED DIET.

~ Fran Lebowitz

I was really surprised to discover how easy it was to lose weight with EFT, and to keep the weight off. I've spent the majority of my life weighing between 20 and 30 pounds more than I do now.

I think that the first step in losing weight with EFT is *readiness*. Am I ready to do whatever it takes to lose weight and keep it off? While even *thinking* about losing weight is a start, it's not the same as being ready – I mean *really* ready – to deal with the emotions that are hidden beneath the fat. That is why diets don't work, because dieting alone won't help you deal with the core issues that cause you to overeat. Most dieters typically lose weight at first, only to gain it all back (and then some).

Two powerful questions to ask yourself: What is the benefit of keeping this extra weight on? What would be harder for me if I were thinner? When you come up with the answers to these questions, you can use EFT to clear these issues for good.

Some of the hidden reasons people report for keeping weight on:

- I can't afford a new wardrobe
- My fat girlfriends would be mad at me
- Men would come on to me
- Women would come on to me
- I would be too weak
- I would draw too much attention
- I might have an affair with someone
- I am too lazy
- I am too old to lose weight
- I might need surgery to get rid of sagging skin
- I might see more wrinkles on my face

After you come up with a reason, or "payoff," for keeping the extra weight, you can use EFT to once and for all clear it from your emotional body.

Let's say your issue for keeping weight on is because you feel as though you can't afford a new wardrobe. Your setup phrase might be: Even though...

- I can't afford a new wardrobe, I deeply and completely love and accept myself.
- I'm afraid if I lost weight my clothes would be too big ...
- I might feel embarrassed wearing clothes that hang on me ...

Tap on your karate chop point while saying the above setup phrases. For tapping on the body, (the chart of tapping points I use is on page 165), you could use the following script (feel free to make any changes in the wording so that it works for you). By the way, I like to tap on both sides of the body simultaneously whenever possible.

First round – (for each round, tap on each point around 7 times):

- Inside the Eyebrows (IE): can't afford a new wardrobe
- Outside the Eyebrows (OE): my clothes won't fit
- Under the Eyes (UE): I don't have money for a new wardrobe
- Under the Nose (UN): can't afford new clothes
- Under the Lip (UL): don't have any extra money
- Collarbone (CB): can't afford new clothes
- Under the Arms (UA): no money for clothes
- Liver Point (LP): no clothes money
- Wrist Points (WP): no extra money
- Top of Head (TH): no clothes money

Second round

- IE: I can't afford a new wardrobe
- OE: but I want to lose weight
- UE: I am tired of being overweight
- UN: but what if I lose weight and don't have the right clothes
- UL: I don't know what I will do
- CB: I can look in my closet and find something that would work for when I lose 10 pounds
- UA: maybe I can start losing weight and figure out what to do after I lose the weight
- LP: I think I can work it out
- WP: I'm not sure how to work it out yet
- TH: I'm not going to let this old story stop me from losing weight

Third round
- IE: my old story was an excuse
- OE: I choose to let go of this extra weight

- UE: I choose to let go of this old story about not being able to afford a wardrobe
- UN: I choose to be aware of all of my feelings around food
- UN: I will remember to tap if I am eating unconsciously
- CB: I know I can do this
- UA: I remember to tap when I feel anxious around food
- LP: I choose to be at my ideal weight and size
- WP: I'll figure out what to do about clothes when I get there
- TH: This is easy!

I may be available (by appointment) to do phone sessions if you get stuck. I have great success at helping people get unstuck. Why wait?

4

Shoulder Pain Disappears in One EFT Session

EFT IS AT THE FOREFRONT OF THE
NEW HEALING MOVEMENT.

~ Candace Pert, PhD

Eileen is a jeweler in her early sixties who has been widowed for several years. She had a chronic pain in her left shoulder that had been bothering her for years. She described it as a dull ache deep in her shoulder joint. She said that it was registering between 6 and 7 on the 0-10 intensity scale.

I asked her what her shoulder would say if it could speak. Eileen reported feelings of inadequacy, fear of being dependent and fears of disability, limitation and aging. She was tired of shouldering responsibilities. She wanted to lay down her burden and release the pain.

Statements that she used while rubbing her tender spot included: Even though ...

- I feel inadequate, I deeply and completely love and accept myself.

- I'm afraid of being dependent …
- I have fear of disability …
- I am afraid of limitation …
- I feel tired of shouldering responsibilities …
- I choose to put down my burden and release whatever is causing this pain in my shoulder …

Some feelings came up, and she had a few tears when she tapped on shouldering responsibilities and putting down her burden. We checked in after tapping and her pain intensity went down to a "3."

Then she tapped using the setup phrase, "Even though I am afraid that if I release this burden I'll crash and burn financially …"

The intensity level soon dropped down to a "1" – where it wasn't even registering as pain but simply as a sensation. I talked to Eileen several months later, and the pain had not returned. She reported feeling so much better that she had returned to swimming several times a week.

5

Clearing the Way for Natural Birth

By REMOVING EMOTIONAL TRAUMA, EFT HELPS
HEAL PHYSICAL SYMPTOMS TOO.
~ Norm Shealy, MD

"Suzie" had about six weeks to go until giving birth. It would be her first child, and she wanted to have it at home. She'd been going through a difficult period with her husband, "Joe," and she also had some major issues about the birth process itself.

I found that conscious breathing and laughter were particularly useful in helping Suzie move energy with EFT. First, we worked on her relationship with her husband. She couldn't figure out how to clearly tell him her needs, and not being telepathic, he couldn't figure out what she wanted. After one round, her intensity level about her husband came down to about a 5. Then she said, Even though …

- I feel upset because Joe doesn't do what I want him to, and I don't tell him what I want him to do, I deeply and completely love and accept myself for not telling him what I want and expect him to do.

- I am really pissed off that Joe can "never" get it right, I deeply and completely love and accept myself for blaming him.
- I just expect Joe to know telepathically what I want him to do ...

She cracked up after saying each "Even though," and the tension visibly drained out of her body. We alternated reminder phrases like "really angry," and "he can't get it right," with lots of laughter. This sequence quickly brought her intensity level down to a 0, so that it was no longer an issue.

Then we dealt with her fear of not being able to have the baby at home (remember, this was her first birth) and of having to go to the hospital. Both of these issues, including her husband not intuitively understanding her needs and of possibly having to go to the hospital, were relatively easy to tap through. When the hour was up, I felt as though there was something deeper to work on. Fortunately, we had some extra time, and she was willing to go for it.

She had been saving the biggest issue, concern about the baby's health, for last. She had gained a lot of weight (she ended up gaining 50 pounds over the course of the pregnancy), and she already had some health issues prior to getting pregnant. When it got right down to it, she was terrified of something horrible happening at the birth. We started tapping on her fear, and it was all blaa, blaa, blaa, a mental exercise that wasn't working. Her intensity stayed at a 10. She got even more worked up as we continued.

I felt as though we needed to do something drastic. I had already talked with Suzie about using colorful language – how with EFT it is more effective to use language that precisely mirrors what we actually say in our own minds. That is why I encourage my clients to change the way I say it if I don't get their language quite right. I often encourage them to cuss, as I've found that it can be extremely helpful to make their affirmations more "colorful." I tested the waters with, "Even though I am terrified that my baby might be fu***ed up, I deeply and completely love and accept myself."

I knew that I had nailed it when every time she said "Fu***ed up baby," she cracked up. Her intensity dropped down to a 0 in one round. All her terror about birthing disappeared by the end of that session, and did not return.

Suzie and her husband were able to have a home birth. When the time came, Suzie didn't have any worries about her baby's health. She was able to tune in to her instincts and follow her internal instructions. She had people assisting at the delivery and she followed her own flow. She birthed naturally in only six hours, just the way she had intended. Their healthy and happy baby is now several years old and doing extremely well, as are the parents.

6

Soothing Abscessed Tooth Pain

WHATEVER YOU'RE THINKING ABOUT IS LITERALLY LIKE
PLANNING A FUTURE EVENT. WHEN YOU'RE WORRYING,
YOU ARE PLANNING. WHEN YOU ARE APPRECIATING, YOU
ARE PLANNING ... WHAT ARE YOU PLANNING?
~ Abraham-Hicks

I retired from my career as a high school teacher in 2006. Before I left, I had begun using EFT with my students. Here is one example of just how quickly it can work, even in a classroom setting.

One day I noticed a student (I'll call her "Mindy") with a pained look on her face. She said she had an abscessed tooth. She had forgotten her medication and couldn't concentrate enough to work on her assignment. Her pain level was 8/10.

We used these statements for the first round: Even though ...

- I have an abscessed tooth, I am an OK kid.
- I forgot my medication ...
- There is throbbing pain up the right side of my face ...
- They might have to pull the tooth out ...

Mindy's pain level dropped to 6/10 after the first round. We had a little more time before the next class, so we did a second round. It dropped some more, down to 4/10. We used the above statements along with "Even though it still hurts ..."

Listening closely, I heard her make a growling noise. I had her continue with the previous statements and had her "GURRRR" louder – which made her giggle, "Even though this throbbing pain is still here, GURRRRR!"

It dropped to a 1/10. One final round brought it to 0.

When I work with a client, I pay particular attention to any vocalizations and encourage my clients to get loud. Also, anytime I can get someone to laugh, it "breaks the ice" of cellular memory.

You may have noticed that in the second part of the setup phrase, we used "I am an OK kid," instead of "I deeply and completely love and accept myself." They both do the same thing, but many youth prefer, "I am an OK kid," or even, "I am an awesome kid."

7

Shingles Pain Disappears

EFT IS DESTINED TO BE A TOP HEALING
TOOL FOR THE 21ST CENTURY.

~ Cheryl Richardson

"Kelsey" had been suffering painful shingles attacks for over three months. She tried strong pain killers, but they made her sick. Not only that, a pharmacist told her that pain medications can cause lasting damage, so she decided she needed to get off of them. Kelsey told me how the stinging pain seemed to come out of nowhere, and that it usually appeared on the right side of her midriff. Some days the intensity level had been a 10/10. On the day of our session, it was "only" a 4/10.

When I asked if anything major happened before her first shingles attack, at first she couldn't think of anything. Then she told me some of what she had been through in the last 13 years. Her husband had become terminally ill, and she had taken care of him for three years. She had quite a story to tell of all that she had been through after his death. Compared to everything she'd been through, it was a quiet and peaceful time – except for the shingles.

It seemed as though we weren't uncovering any issues that were related to her *present* condition. Then a thought just popped into my head. "Is there anybody that has *gotten under your skin?*" I asked. Kelsey pondered the question for a bit. She shared about a nice man she had dated five years previously who she still felt sad about breaking up with. She wished it could have gone further than it did, but his daughter "Joyce" had become an issue.

At first, Kelsey was quite fond of Joyce. However, there had been a situation in which she was invited to a family event, and Joyce had acted *like a baby*. The way she acted toward Kelsey's family was totally unacceptable. After that incident, Kelsey cut Joyce out of her life. She said that she had worked on being distant (as a way to get back at Joyce). At the time of the incident, her anger was off the chart. Today, it was still a "5," and Kelsey was surprised to discover that she still carried a charge. She really thought that she had handled her emotions around the situation with Joyce, but clearly she had not.

We tapped on Kelsey's anger with Joyce's father for just brushing it off. We tapped on how unacceptable Joyce's behavior was to Kelsey. We tapped for about 10 minutes without stopping. I fed back all of the stuff she told me about what a *Drama Queen* Joyce was – that she was a big baby; how pissed off Kelsey was; and how resentful she still felt. After finding out that she didn't mind cussing, I sprinkled in a few cuss words and got the laughter flowing.

I asked Kelsey to close her eyes, go within, and then describe the intensity level of her anger. She said it was down to a "2." Kelsey had said that Joyce was rude, and that her behavior was inexcusable. For the last couple of rounds I had her tap on forgiving herself for allowing Joyce to get under her skin, and that it was OK to just let Joyce be the way she is. When we stopped tapping she said, "I feel lighter than air." Her anger intensity dropped to 0. I asked her what level her shingle pain was now (it had been a "4" when we started), and with more than a touch of wonder in her voice she replied that it was gone, too.

We did all of this in one hour. Kelsey didn't even know what EFT was (her friend had given her a free session). I was able to explain to her where to tap (she didn't have a computer, so she couldn't see an EFT tapping chart online).

It was quite a gift to be able to facilitate another amazing transformation. I so love what I (and you, and anyone) can do with EFT!

Dissolving Highway Panic

I SEE EFT CURE THINGS THAT ARE
INCURABLE ALL THE TIME.

~ Eric Robins, MD

The phone rang, and when I answered I was surprised to hear the voice of my sister-in-law, Eileen, who was on her way down for a family get together. She had been planning on coming to our gathering for a couple of months, and we were expecting her. She called from a rest stop about half way here, and she didn't think she could drive any farther. Between deep, racking sobs she explained her situation.

Eileen, in her mid-sixties and living alone, was carrying several gallons of water out to her car when she slipped. Afraid that she would fall on her face, she was able to catch herself, but in doing so, she pulled a muscle in her right leg. Even though she really hurt her leg, she thought she would be OK to drive.

Unfortunately, the pain got worse as she drove. Three hours into her trip, she made her plea to me by cell phone. The pain was so bad in her right leg she couldn't put her foot on the accelerator. She had to use cruise control to drive. Eileen feared that she couldn't even get to a motel relatively close by, let alone drive another 150 miles.

Cutting to the chase, I asked her to tell me about her emotional state. She reported feeling embarrassed and clumsy because she had almost fallen, as well as disappointed that she might not be able to make it to our gathering. Fearful that she might be stranded at the rest stop, Eileen told me that she was feeling despair because she didn't know if she could even make it back home. Panicked, Eileen didn't know what to do.

Following EFT Master Lindsay Kenny's "bundling baggage" concept (see glossary), I helped Eileen bundle together disappointment, fear, panic, and embarrassment. I asked her what she might title the past three hours if it was a movie, and she replied, "Stumble Bum." She rated her bundle of emotions at a 7/10. She said that the intensity had gone down because she was picking up on my calmness and certainty that we could clear up this situation.

Some of the setup phrases we used included: Even though ...

- I feel panicked because I can't drive, I deeply and completely love and accept myself.
- I feel disappointed that I may not make it to dinner tonight with my family ...
- I feel embarrassed that I slipped and hurt myself ...

Her first reminder phrase was, "I feel panicked." Then we alternated the following reminder phrases:

- I feel so disappointed ...
- I'm afraid I might be stuck here ...

- Stumble Bum …
- I feel embarrassed …

After three or four rounds, I asked Eileen how she felt, and she replied that she no longer felt panicked. I could hear the hope in her voice. What was left, she continued, was a pounding in her heart with an intensity level between 3 and 4. She added that she still felt disappointed and embarrassed. We did a couple more rounds and added a few cuss words to lighten it up. Her intensity level dropped to a 2. We did another round about her disappointment and her intensity level went to a 1.

When we started, the pain in her right leg was at a 6, and it dropped as the emotional intensity lessened. The pain went from 6 to 4. Then it dropped to 3, and Eileen said her leg was no longer an issue.

Eileen announced that she was going to see me at dinner, and she did just that. She was able to drive three more hours with minimal discomfort. I was so happy to see her smiling face when I arrived at the restaurant.

Armed with knowledge about how to get to core issues hiding beneath physical pain, I was able to help my beloved friend go from complete panic and debilitating pain to being able to drive another three hours, and most importantly, for her to be able to make it to an important family event.

9

Homeless Man's Backache Vanishes

BESIDES WORKING WELL ON PSYCHOLOGICAL TRAUMAS,
EFT HAS ESTABLISHED A SURPRISING TRACK RECORD
OF EFFECTIVENESS IN SHIFTING, OR EVEN
CURING, PHYSICAL AILMENTS.

~ Dawson Church

I had gone to town to run some errands and do a little Christmas shopping. My last stop was at our local co-op, and in front of the store a young man approached me asking for money. "Ira" said that he was in a lot of pain. I told him that I thought I could help him – *if* he was interested.

He had been in a car accident about a year before – he said that he had been going 100 miles an hour when he ran into a tree. His body was still wracked with pain. His back ached in several places, his wrist had been broken, and he had metal pins holding some bones together. He also had a large scar on his face from the accident. When he agreed to let me help him make the pain go away, I suggested that we go around the corner of the store, so not as many people would be staring at us.

I asked if he was familiar with acupuncture, and he nodded. I told him that what we were going to do was like acupuncture, but without needles. Then I asked what was hurting the most. He mentioned his lower back. I asked about the intensity, and he said that right now it was "only" a 7/10, though he had to lean up against the wall for added support.

His setup phrases were: Even though …

- My back really hurts, I deeply and completely love and accept myself.
- My back hurts like hell …

We completed one full round. His reminder phrase was, "really hurts." After that round, I asked how his pain was, and he said that it was a little better, down to about a 6. He said that the cold really made it worse, and I saw his eyes tearing up. It was December, and he was unsheltered. It had been getting well below freezing at night.

His next setup phrases included, Even though:

- My back really hurts …
- The cold makes my back hurt even more …
- My back hurts like hell …

When we cussed, he laughed. We continued tapping with the reminder phrase "hurts like hell," and "the cold makes it worse." I added in a few additional cuss words to make him laugh some more. That brought his intensity level down to a 4. Another round brought it down to a 2. We did one final round which brought it down to a 0.

Afraid to move because he thought that the pain would come back, Ira stepped carefully away from the wall. He looked surprised. He still didn't have any pain in his back. His face lit up! I reviewed the process with him, so he would be able to use it in the future. We wished each other a Merry Christmas before he wandered back to the front of the store to continue panhandling.

10

Tapping Away my Hunger Headache

EFT IS THE SURPRISING NATURAL HEALING AID
YOU CAN USE FOR ALMOST EVERYTHING.

~ Gary Craig

If you really knew me, you'd know that sometimes I neglect my personal needs. The other day, for example, I didn't eat as much food as my body needed. So, there I was, a passenger in the car being driven by my husband to the coast, and I started getting a headache because I hadn't eaten enough. I really didn't feel like talking about it with my husband, so I started silently tapping on my karate chop point to see if I could get some relief.

Some of the setup phrases were: Even though ...

- I have a headache that was probably caused because I haven't eaten enough food today, I deeply and completely love and accept myself.
- I know better than to go this long between meals ...
- I am angry at myself for not taking better care of my body and I am paying for it now ...

- I am sabotaging myself by not taking care of my needs …
- I feel stupid for not taking care of myself …

It worked! I ended up feeling better – even though I worked on this silently.

~ TIP ~

No one needs to know that you are doing EFT. You can squeeze the karate chop point on the side of your hand while you are saying your setup phrase.

Also, many times we have a "sweet spot." You may notice that you favor a certain point, and that you tap there more than on other points. That is your sweet spot. Some people call it a "hot spot." If you are in a situation in which you don't want people to know you are doing EFT, you can discreetly massage or press your sweet spot while silently repeating your setup and reminder phrases.

Something else that works well is to *imagine* that you are tapping your different points. With your mind's eye, you can go tap, tap, tap… (about 7 times) on each point. While you're mentally tapping, it's a good idea to remember to focus on what your issue or emotion is – so that you don't space out.

11

How I Avoided a Nasty Bruise

USE EFT TO HELP DISSOLVE FEELINGS OF DESPERATION.

~ Joe Vitale

My husband and I went to a friend's retirement party. My husband put together some great music from the 60s and 70s for all of us to dance to. Towards the end of the party, another woman and I decided to spin each other. We held hands and pivoted, pulling our heads back to gain momentum. Laughing like crazy, we spun faster and faster.

My inner child was having a blast when suddenly the other woman's shoe slipped off her foot. She lost her balance and fell down, with me tumbling after her. I slammed into the thinly carpeted cement floor with my left hip. Ouch! That hurt like hell. I felt pretty stupid and I was afraid that I might have broken my hip. Slowly, I was able to turn myself over and get up on my hands and knees, then tentatively stood up and hobbled into the bathroom. Behind the closed door in the stall I started to use EFT. I tapped for the excruciating pain in my hip and for feeling stupid and embarrassed. The intensity level of my pain was a 7-8.

Here are a few of the setup phrases I used: Even though …

- I feel really stupid for spinning so fast and falling down on the hard floor, I deeply and completely love and accept myself.
- My left hip hurts like hell …
- It looks like where I hit my hip is turning into a big yellow bruise …
- Someone my age shouldn't be doing something as dangerous as spinning really fast …
- It was incredibly fun until we hit the hard floor …
- People may have thought I was crazy …
- I feel embarrassed for acting like a kid …
- I feel like an idiot …
- I feel grateful that I didn't break my hip …

Tapping for about ten minutes brought the intensity level of my pain down to a 3-4. My husband, Steve, drove us home after the party, and I tapped again using some of the above setup phrases. The next day I tapped some more, and also tapped for feeling stiff.

After four days, I never did get a bruise (I tend to bruise relatively easily). I couldn't feel any pain unless I touched the area that I landed on, and then it felt a little tender. Thanks to EFT, I didn't get a bruise!

12

Angry Wife Clears Headache and Cramps

I HAVE BEEN USING EFT FOR YEARS AND HAVE FOUND IT
A PIVOTAL TOOL IN CREATING THE LIFE OF MY DREAMS.
                                            ~ Jack Canfield

"Elizabeth" came in for a session and I asked her what she wanted to
work on. She complained about menopausal symptoms. On this day
she was experiencing a headache and menstrual cramps. Her headache
intensity level was a 6 and her menstrual cramps intensity was a 7.

After talking with Elizabeth, I found that her main concern was
that she was under a lot of stress. She felt as though she needed to
get more child support from her ex-husband. She was running out
of money to buy food and other necessities for the kids before the
end of the month. The main emotion she was feeling was anger
at her ex-husband for not giving them the support she felt they
deserved. Her intensity level was a 10.

Some of Elizabeth's setup phrases included: Even though …

- I am really angry at my ex-husband for being a jerk, I deeply and completely love and accept myself.
- I am pissed off at my ex-husband for cheating me out of money that I need for my kids …
- I am angry at myself for stuffing my anger because it isn't good for me to leak it out on my kids, students or innocent bystanders … and I forgive myself! I really have been doing the best I know how.

While she tapped, I had her inhale deeply, then forcefully exhale her anger. Then she tapped on her points for four rounds and brought her intensity level down to a 6. I asked about her cramps, and they had disappeared. Her headache had shifted to a different spot, and the intensity level dropped from a 6 to a 4. She commented that she could actually feel the anger dissipating out of the soles of her feet.

I explained how pain moving around usually means that the initial issue had cleared, and there was something else to deal with. I asked Elizabeth what she intuited that "something else" to be, and she replied that she had become aware of what a waste of energy and time her anger at her ex had become.

The new setup phrases that we used were: Even though …

- I still have this intensity level 6 anger and it is a waste of energy, I deeply and completely love and accept myself, and forgive myself for focusing so much on this anger.
- Though I am still pissed off at my ex, I can see that it is a waste of energy …

I had her tap on the anger, and what a waste of time it was. She did a couple of rounds very loudly, focusing on her breath and cussing up a storm. As she got the anger out, I noticed that there had been a shift. I started using the Choices Method (see glossary), having her say, "I choose to notice when I get angry." I could tell from the slight frown on her brow that she wasn't quite ready to embrace that. I had her follow with, "No, I don't," in a little girl's voice – tap, tap, tap. "I don't think I can do that yet" – tap, tap, tap. "Yes, I can" – tap, tap, tap. "No, I can't" – tap, tap, tap. As her face lightened she began to giggle.

While we were tapping, I included, "I will notice when I get angry" – tap, tap, tap. "Then I will inhale and go to my center and exhale"– tap, tap, tap. "Then I will choose what I am going to do"– tap, tap, tap. "If I am angry, I will feel my anger, and I will let it go"– tap, tap, tap. "I will notice, choose and act"– tap, tap, tap. This brought her anger intensity level down to a 2. I asked about her headache and she blinked in astonishment, reporting that it had disappeared. All that remained was just a little tightness in her temples.

We then tapped on the Gamut Point (see Tapping Chart on page 165) on the top of her hand. I had Elizabeth roll her eyes as she hummed and counted. Most of the time when I use EFT, I do a simplified version that doesn't include the 9 Gamut Procedure. In this case, however, I did, because it helps balance the left and right hemispheres of the brain. When using this technique, tap on the Gamut Point while rolling your eyes, humming and counting. (For a more thorough explanation of the 9 Gamut Procedure, please see the Glossary.) Using this procedure brought the intensity level of her anger down to a 0.

We did all of this in about 45 minutes. Elizabeth learned a new strategy for when she feels angry. Instead of carrying her anger with her and wasting a lot of energy, she can *notice* that she is angry, and then *choose* what to do. One choice is to tap the anger out – to *act* rather than carrying it around and wasting energy. Elizabeth learned that she could truly be free from being stuck in an emotional black hole.

13

A Year of Backaches Disappears in ONE Session

IT IS NOT ENOUGH TO DESIRE SOMETHING.
ANYONE WHO IS UNABLE TO CLEAR BASIC BLOCKS
TO SUCCESS WILL REMAIN "STUCK." NO TECHNIQUE
COMES CLOSE TO THE POWER OF EFT FOR CLEARING
LIMITING BELIEFS AND MOVING YOU TOWARDS
YOUR GOALS, FINANCIAL OR OTHERWISE.

~ Carol Look

Although "Carry" appeared to be in her early 20s, I found out later that she was 37. She said that her L-5 disk was bulging in her lower back, and that she was in constant pain. She had injured her back about a year before, though she wasn't quite sure how it had happened. Since her work required her to lift objects and be quite active, that is probably how it occurred. Carry assumed that she had just overdone it.

The year before, she had gone to Reggae on the River and had "indulged" in a lot of drugs while she was there. Reflecting back on her behavior, she felt as though she had acted like she had when she was much younger, and that she was paying for it. She had done way too much dancing and staying up late, and had not rested enough before going back to work. Consequently, when she returned to work she was exhausted, but she still had much to do, and that was when she hurt her back. Here it was almost one year later and it *still* hurt. Carry complained that her back pain was at a 4-5 level – like a constant stretch.

I asked Carry if there could be any secondary benefits from her back being out of whack. Her eyebrows shot up, clearly intrigued by that question. She had already told me a couple of things that could be secondary benefits. She couldn't scrub too hard or perform other tasks such as bending or lifting. Since she had been making a living as a housekeeper, she realized that she needed to look at her future and what she wanted to do with her life. So, in that way, she felt as though the pain in her back was a gift. It had opened her eyes to the possibility of changing her career to one of the healing arts.

I told Carry that her back pain probably had to do with some emotions that she had stored in her body. Six months earlier she had broken up with her boyfriend and still felt a lot of anxiety, sadness and hurt – her intensity level was 10/10. After a few rounds of tapping, we were able to get it down to a 7-8. Her heavy heart brightened a bit, but I felt as though there was something bigger than her feelings around her ex-boyfriend, and explained how important it was to get to the root of her emotions.

With coaxing, I was able to get her to go back in time and revisit some old emotional pain. She shared that she had recently lost her grandmother, mother, father, grandfather, and her cat of 25 years. Her brother had AIDS, her other brother was a mess, she had divorced after a 12-year marriage, and she had another cat with the same problem as the cat that she had to put down.

In other words, Carry had lots of loss in her life. I asked her, if she could give that period of time when she had so much loss a title – like a television series – what would it be? The first thing that came to her mind was "S**t." The other word was "Life."

So, we tapped on her "S**t Life" and the anxiety, sadness, grief, and hurt that she felt. We did lots of rounds on this black heaviness buried in her head as well as her heart. The intensity of her feelings was at a 10. We were able to get it down to a 7-8 level. I could see that we needed to be more specific with her grief and sadness.

The loss of her grandparents was really big for her. They were her security. When she thought about their deaths, her grief was a 10. We tapped with continuous rounds. I noticed that every time I threw in "s**t" or "sh**ty life" she would laugh and lighten up. So, I made sure to add s**t to all of the rounds. I asked how she addressed her grandparents, and she replied, "Granny and Grand-daddy" (I feel that it is good to speak the same way as the client). Her intensity level wasn't dropping, and then she revealed that, "I wished I could have been at Granddaddy's death – I tried to get there, but I missed it." We tapped on the guilt she felt about miss-ing his death. We couldn't get below a 6-7.

Then Carry uncovered another layer surrounding her grandpar-ents' death. Her aunt Georgia had falsely accused Carry of taking some of her Granny's things. Aunt Georgia turned Carry's family against her, and she felt betrayed. Her intensity level was a 10 on her feelings of being betrayed by Aunt Georgia, and cut off from her family. We were able to bring her intensity level down to a 4.

I had worked up quite a sweat. Almost two hours had passed, and I was running out of steam. Carry had a story that all of this stuff had been with her for 16 years, and that it was going to take time to get rid of it. I reminded her that s**t could go in one big dump. She didn't have to stay constipated with these feelings all of her life. We did one last round of tapping on letting go of the s**t that was no longer serving her.

Then I asked Carry how her back was doing. Surprised, she replied that the pain had disappeared. Carry pointed out that she had been sitting on a backless stool for almost two hours, yet the constant pain in her back for the past year was now gone!

14

Using EFT for Exercise Motivation

TAPPING BRINGS CHOICE BACK INTO YOUR LIFE.
YOU CHOOSE HOW YOU WANT TO FEEL AND WHAT
YOU WANT TO LET GO OF. YOU'RE IN CONTROL!
~ Nick Ortner

During the summer of 2005, I had the pure joy of being able to hang out with our goddaughter, Kamala. A couple of months old at the time, I had the enormous pleasure of holding that sweet bundle of joy! To my dismay, it really hurt my elbows, wrists and hands to hold her. In fact, a couple of times I felt as though I was in danger of dropping her, that my joints simply couldn't handle her weight.

I have been dealing with Lyme disease for decades. My symptoms have included aching joints and not having much strength in my hands. I was concerned, not only because it was difficult to hold my goddaughter, but because within six months I was going to become a grandmother. How would I be able to safely hold my grandchild?

As a former PE teacher and athlete, I knew the importance of exercise – especially lifting weights. Yet when would I ever fit exercising into my busy schedule? I had been doing a lot of reading about EFT, and I had been using it with my friends and family. Could EFT help me get back in shape? Out of my desire to safely hold my grandchild, I decided to get up a little bit earlier and exercise. I used the following setup phrases while tapping on several of my body's tapping points (also known as energy meridians).

Even though ...

- I don't feel like getting out of bed to exercise, I deeply and completely love and accept myself.
- I feel like I would rather sleep instead of getting up to exercise ...
- I don't feel like I can stick with an exercise program ...
- I don't feel like I can pull this off ...
- I don't feel like exercising ...
- I hate lifting weights ...
- I feel stupid using little weights ...

Several months later, I continued to exercise at least five days a week. I started out using a hula-hoop just to make it more fun. Then, I typically jumped on a mini-trampoline three times a week, and did my weight lifting routine for two days. On days that I didn't feel like getting out of bed to exercise, I would do some EFT while I lay in bed. Then I would be able to get up and move my body! The bottom line: Tessa is now over four years old, and I have never had a problem holding her (although I must admit she's getting pretty heavy).

15

Father-to-be Releases Stress

WHEN YOU FEEL GOOD THOUGHTS, HAPPY THOUGHTS,
IT'S A COMPLETELY DIFFERENT SET OF CHEMICALS
THAN WHEN YOU'RE FEELING ANGRY OR HOPELESS.
~ Dr. Daniel Amen

The following story beautifully illustrates my contention that *intent* is the single most important tool in successfully using EFT. During that stressful time just before the baby arrived, first-time father-to-be "Joe" often felt that his wife's requests were unreasonable, and he would notice his anger surge. (You may remember Joe and Suzie from chapter 5.) Using the principles of EFT, Joe developed a simple yet potent strategy for creatively releasing his anger.

Joe and I had done an EFT session a few months previously, but Joe had forgotten the details of where to tap. During the final week before the baby came, both parents-to-be were (understandably) dealing with a lot of stress. Joe had been finishing up last minute projects around the house and he felt stretched to the max. Suzie was tired of having the baby inside of her. She was ready to have it out – *now*.

According to Joe, Suzie was not acting reasonably. (That is the way of it. Women are not reasonable at this particular time.) When he felt as though she was being unreasonable, he would get out of her sight (instead of getting into a squabble with her and making her wrong) and start tapping.

The only tapping point that Joe could remember was the top of his head. He told me that he had been pounding the top of his head like a drum while loudly complaining about his wife's behavior. Since he made sure that he got out of her space, he was able to get loud, bitching and moaning and tapping the top of his head until it tingled.

The result? He was able to stay relatively calm, considering that his wife was feeling all her emotions while having their first baby (at home, no less). Fortunately, she had already used EFT to clear away all of her fears about birth, and after labor started, it only lasted six hours.

When I asked Joe about his experience of the birth, he said that it was his intent that had helped him to stay calm. Even though he was too excited to remember any other points besides the top of his head, it ended up working like a charm. Ultimately, his intent was more important than which (or how many) points he tapped.

16

Batting Average Soars

MOST SPORTS PEOPLE WOULD AGREE THAT SUCCESS STARTS
IN THE MIND, AND THIS IS WHERE EFT DOES THE WORK.

~ Sejual Shah

A few minutes were left in my high school art class. Alex asked if I could help him with his .280 batting average. Since class was almost over, I told him that we had time to do only one round. He quickly told me what he felt was making it hard for him to succeed.

It turns out that in modern times, a seasonal batting average higher than .300 is considered to be excellent, with an average higher than .400 a nearly impossible goal (from Wikipedia).

For his setup phrases: Even though ...

- I might strike out, I'm an OK kid.
- I might be too cocky ...
- I have had an off-balance swing ...
- I might not hit the top ...
- I'm afraid of swinging and missing ...
- I've been in a slump ...

He tapped and alternated reminder phrases (while breathing deeply):

- Striking out
- Hit a home run
- Too cocky
- Hit a home run
- Off-balanced swing
- Good hitter
- Swinging and missing
- Home run

He only had one game left in the season, and he hit 3 out of 5 or .600! He made that incredible improvement with just one round of EFT (while students were putting their things away and getting ready to leave class).

17

Hand-Washing Compulsion Dissolves in Minutes

WHEN A REVOLUTIONARY NEW TECHNIQUE OR
THERAPY IS DESCRIBED, IT CAN TAKE A WHILE
FOR SCIENCE TO CATCH UP.

~ Dawson Church, PhD

"Linda" worked in the sales department of a local advertiser. She said that she washed her hands all the time, and that it had become both annoying and distracting. She would wash her hands at least 50 times a day, and she wanted to let go of that behavior. We determined that washing her hands was at an intensity level of 7/10 in terms of the behavior being a compulsion. We started with: Even though …

- I am compulsive about washing my hands, I deeply and completely love and accept myself.
- I wash my hands more than I need to …

Then she mentioned that the front doorknob was disgusting, and when she entered this building (we were at her job site) she always had to wash her hands. We tapped for that, but her intensity level didn't go down. Linda told me that she had been battling with cancer and that was when she acquired the hand-washing behavior. We added: Even though I have been washing my hands because I don't want my cancer to get worse, I deeply and completely love and accept myself.

Then I asked her to go out to the front door and look at the disgusting doorknob to determine her anxiety level. She was surprised to see that her anxiety level had dropped to a 4/10. Then we did another round, adding: Even though ...

- I'm tired of washing my hands so much ...
- I have been washing my hands to make my cancer go away ...

I asked her to go back to the front door one more time to see how she felt now about touching the doorknob. Her anxiety level had dropped to 2/10. I asked her if she'd like to get it to a 0 and she enthusiastically said, "Yes!" We continued by alternating the following statements: Even though ...

- I still have some anxiety about washing my hands ...
- I now have a healthy attitude about washing my hands ...

I asked her to go back and look at the disgusting doorknob again and see how she felt. She didn't hesitate about opening the door. Her intensity level had dropped to a 0! She also commented on how energetic she felt.

18

Conquering Bothersome Noises

THE WAY TOWARDS FREEDOM FROM A SITUATION
OFTEN LIES IN ACCEPTANCE OF THE SITUATION.
~Rachel Naomi Remen, MD

The other day, I called my daughter-in-love (some say daughter-in-law), Stacey, to see if I could take my granddaughter, Tessa, for a swim. Stacey enthusiastically agreed, and I looked forward to taking Tessa to the pool.

When I arrived at Stacey's, she was returning from a walk with Tessa. I recalled that my husband and I had baby-sat Tessa just a few days before, and she had been returning from a walk then as well. On each occasion there had been a group of teens across the street on skateboards. Stacey complained that they were making a lot of noise until at least 10 p.m. The grinding of the skateboard wheels on the street seemed particularly harsh. The noise had become too much for Stacey, and she started going for lots of walks to get away from it.

We sat in front of Stacey's and had a chat. She told me that she was really having a hard time with the skaters across the street.

The family that had moved in five months previously had teenagers who were into skateboarding. She was so upset about the noise that she pointed to a real estate magazine and said that they were thinking about finding another home. She also mentioned that the new owner was a lawyer.

I told Stacey about some of the wonderful healing results I'd had using EFT, and asked if she would be interested in applying it to see if it could help with her distress. Stacey agreed to give it a try. As we worked, sometimes Tessa copied us by tapping on herself (very cute).

The main feeling that Stacey came up with was frustration. She said that the intensity level of her frustration was 10/10. Some of the setup phrases we used included: Even though …

- I feel so frustrated that those kids skate for hours and hours on end, I deeply and completely love and accept myself.
- I feel frustrated and upset because I feel helpless about them skating all of the time …
- I feel frustrated and helpless about the kids making noise …
- I feel frustrated that my new neighbor is a lawyer and he doesn't seem to be reasonable …

This was not a quick fix. Her intensity level remained high. We went for a ride in the "way-back machine" and found a time when she felt really frustrated and humiliated in high school and tapped on that. It brought her intensity level down a little, though she reported that is was still a 9/10.

I asked her how she knew that her intensity level was still a 9/10, and she said that she still felt *very* frustrated. I asked if she could feel it in her body. "Yes," she replied, though the heaviness she'd talked about had moved out of her chest. The pain had also started to move, and so we followed it.

I am so glad I remembered to ask that important question about where Stacey was currently feeling pain. When the pain starts to move, it often means that the issue being addressed has been cleared, and that another, deeper issue is coming up for healing (see "Chasing the Pain" in the Glossary). Stacey reported feeling a tightness, almost a clenching, in her stomach. I asked, "If your stomach could speak, what would it say?"

With her eyes closed, Stacey contemplated the question for a few seconds before almost shouting, "Stop the noise!" Her intensity level fell to 7/10. Then I talked vividly about the sound of the skateboards grinding on the street late at night, and brought her intensity level back to 10/10. Just thinking about the sound of the skateboard wheels had touched a raw nerve.

Stacey recognized how helpless and angry she felt with the situation. She loved returning from work to the quietness of her home. This was the way she recharged her batteries – being at home where it is peaceful (she teaches school during the day). Some of the setup phrases we came up with included: Even though …

- I feel really angry that the kids across the street don't care for anybody except themselves …
- I feel angry that the skaters woke me up, and that they didn't even seem to care about anybody but themselves …
- I feel pissed off that those "immature little kids" (this brought out a laugh), those "little brats," are totally unaware that they are keeping me up … and I forgive myself, and I forgive those little brats for being so immature.

We tapped on how helpless she felt. Even though she had been writing letters and joining with others in her neighborhood, she felt that because the guy across the street was a lawyer, they weren't going to be very successful. We tapped on her fear of having to sell the home she loved so much.

Next we tapped for Stacey to be able to mentally turn the volume down when she heard the grinding skateboard wheels, so it wouldn't bother her in the same way. We also tapped on her being able to stay centered even through the grating skateboard noise. The goal was for her to be able to go to that peaceful place inside that no one could touch no matter what was going on.

We were able to get her intensity level down to 5/10. I asked how she knew it was a 5, and she said that the tightness in her stomach had disappeared. About an hour and a half had flown by since we started. She told me that, just like her husband (my son), I was very persistent. With a smile, I asked her, "Where do you think he got it from?"

I called her the next day. She thanked me profusely. She felt as though she could finally eat, because her stomach had relaxed. The tightness that had been there for months was gone. A few days later she added that the lawyer had sent out a conciliatory letter, and that a workable compromise finally appeared within reach. Stacey's relief was palpable.

19

Lawyer's Skin Condition Improves

As WE SHIFT OUR EMOTIONAL STATES, WE SHIFT OUR
BASIC BODY CHEMISTRY. IF WE SHIFT FROM A LESS
HEALTHY EMOTION TO A HEALTHIER EMOTION,
WE SHIFT OUR BODY CHEMISTRY IN THE
DIRECTION OF HEALTH.

– O. Carl Simonton, MD

I recently met a young man at a meeting in San Francisco. I heard him complain that he'd been dealing with a skin condition for over four months, and that he had been to several doctors and specialists, to no avail. I told him about my energy work, and that if he was interested in trying something different to give me a call. A couple of weeks later he made an appointment.

"Theodore" told me that he wasn't exactly sure what had caused the skin eruptions on the backs of his hands. He thought perhaps that it was a lingering case of poison oak, and that he may have gotten it from his cats, but it didn't heal. The next month it spread to his face. One doctor prescribed steroids, and the condition seemed to go away, though after he stopped taking the steroids his condition came back, only worse. He had a full body rash, and his skin was extremely dry. According to him, he thought that his immune system was in overdrive.

I found out that Theodore had only recently become a lawyer, and that he felt as though he had taken on too much responsibility. He shared that he had both work-related and personal issues. He had broken up with his girlfriend a little over a year ago, and he missed the connection. He had endured an outbreak on his hands right before his girlfriend moved out.

Since he was a new lawyer, he felt obligated to take on everything – even if he didn't like the case. He felt as though he had been taken advantage of because he was the new guy, and he felt bombarded by pleas for help from all directions. It was also stressful for him to deal with all of the egos and agendas in the office.

When I asked Theodore how he liked being a lawyer, he answered that he was questioning the nature of the work that he was doing. I am always looking for any conflict that my clients feel they are in, and he felt both trapped and confined. Though being a lawyer was the path he had chosen, he now felt locked into it. His level of intensity was a 9-10. Here are some of the setup phrases he used: Even though …

- I feel trapped and confined as a lawyer, I deeply and completely love and accept myself.
- I spent all of this time and money on becoming a lawyer and my family expects me to follow through …
- I feel like I am locked into a career where there are parts of it that I really hate …

After one round of tapping, Theodore's intensity level dropped to 6/10. The muscles of his lower back began to relax. He felt a gentleness that he hadn't experienced in a long while. He confided that he wanted his parents to love him. His next batch of setup phrases included: Even though ...

- I feel trapped because I am practicing law and I dislike a lot of what I see, and I feel uncomfortable being in some of the situations that I have been in ... and I forgive myself for getting into situations that I find unacceptable.
- There is a part of me that hates being a lawyer and dealing with ass hole lawyers and unreasonable clients ...
- I have overextended myself and have been a patsy – and that has not felt good – my skin has been trying to tell me that it doesn't like how I have been handling these different situations, and I deeply and completely love and accept that my skin has been trying to tell me to say "no" to some of these arrangements, and I promise my system that I will pay attention to how I feel. I forgive myself for raging a war inside my body.

These setup phrases and tapping on the points on Theodore's face and torso brought his intensity level down to 3/10. It was amazing to see how much more relaxed he looked, including the muscles in his jaw. Then I started to balance positive and negative affirmations: Even though ...

- I haven't known what to do, and my skin has been telling me that things aren't right inside, when I get in a situation where I feel uncomfortable, I remember to breathe and go to my center. Here I can make the right decisions ...
- I have been uncomfortable with taking on too much in my first year practicing law, I will now remember to be aware of how I am feeling. I remember to breathe and center. I am whole and complete.

- I have had a tough first year being a lawyer, I have learned a lot. I know my limits and pay attention to how I feel. I breathe, let go and become present.

As Theodore tapped on his face points, he started laughing at the absurdity of his situation. After one round, it had already dropped to a 1/10. He said that he was enjoying the lightness and love in his heart. We did one more round of tapping, this time all positive:

- I am in my heart
- I am in the present moment
- I know exactly what to do
- I take on the right amount of work for myself
- I am an honest lawyer
- I serve the people
- I balance work and play
- I have fun

This brought his intensity level down to 0. Theodore seemed totally relaxed, yet vibrant. The swelling in his hands went down and they no longer itched. I telephoned him a few days later to see how things were going. He said that his hands were even better, and he felt great!

20

Relieving Tax Stress

SO OFTEN TIME IT HAPPENS,

WE ALL LIVE OUR LIFE IN CHAINS,

AND WE NEVER EVEN KNOW WE HAVE THE KEY.

~The Eagles, "Already Gone"

"Cindy" had been a client for several months. On her last visit she told me that she hadn't dealt with her taxes for three years. She complained that the "State" was after her, and feared that she wouldn't have enough money to pay her taxes. Cindy confessed that she had resistance to making an appointment to see the tax preparer. She said that she needed to have her tax return finished and turned in by April 15 – one month and one day away, and she hadn't even made an appointment yet.

Cindy's anxiety level was about a 4 when she thought about doing her taxes. Then I asked her about making an appointment with a tax person, and her anxiety level shot up to a 7.

I asked Cindy if she had experienced feeling something like this in her past (other than the times that she was slow at getting her taxes in) where she felt the same kind of fear, anxiety and procrastination. She replied that when she was in college, she had a problem finishing up her Senior Project, and admitted that she had a serious problem with procrastination. She put off working on her Senior Project until the last minute, and as a result received a lower grade. Back when she was in college, her anxiety around not doing the project and getting it in on time had been a 10. However, when she reflected on how she put off her Senior Project, her dominant emotion was disappointment, with an intensity of 4.

We tapped on her disappointment for putting off doing her Senior Project, and her fear of doing it wrong. Cindy had a rough time with her father when she was growing up, so I suggested that she had a problem not just with her father's authority, but *any* authority, including her teachers. Then I pointed out that the State and the Feds are also authorities. We did the argumentative approach for several rounds in which she repeated, "I want to turn my project in," "No, I don't," "Yes, I do," and a few, "You can't make me!" We were able to get her disappointment about procrastinating on her Senior Project down to a 0, and she finally was able to laugh about it.

Then I asked how anxious she felt about making an appointment with the tax preparer, and her anxiety had dropped from a 7 to a 2. At this point she added, "I only have one tax return and it has to be done on time – no choice." However, she still wasn't comfortable making an appointment. So, we did the 9 Gamut Procedure, alternating "I hate authority," and "You can't make me!" as her reminder phrases. After that, she said she didn't feel anxious about seeing the tax man. So, after three years of putting off doing her taxes, Cindy did make an appointment to see her tax person, and followed through with having her taxes completed and sending them in to the IRS.

21

Stroke Symptoms Abate

IF YOU DON'T LIKE SOMETHING CHANGE IT; IF YOU CAN'T
CHANGE IT, CHANGE THE WAY YOU THINK ABOUT IT.
                                    ~Mary Engelbreit

"Jim," 48 years old at the time I saw him, had suffered a stroke about
six months previously. Living out in the country, he lay collapsed on
the floor until he remembered a friend's phone number and called
for help. After the call, Jim lost track of time and didn't have any idea
that he had been on the floor for over 12 hours. He kept picking at
his limp left arm, thinking it was one of his dog's legs.

Finally, some neighbors who had been alerted by a friend came over
and took Jim to the hospital. He was then sent by helicopter to a
big-city hospital that could better handle his situation. Jim spent a
month there before being transferred to a rehabilitation center. He
eventually graduated from rehab when he was able to get up off the
floor by himself. It had been a *very* serious stroke.

At the time I saw him, Jim was living in town in a friend's apart-
ment. He decided that he didn't want to be in a wheelchair any
more, and began to move around carefully with a cane. He couldn't

feel his left leg, but he said it helped support him. His left arm had been partially paralyzed from the stroke, and it rested in a sling with his fingers twisted into a knot. Though the stroke didn't seem to affect his speech or his thought processes, the entire left side of his body was deeply altered.

I asked him to rate the tightness in his left hand, and he replied that it was a 9/10. He couldn't actually move his left arm independently, so he used his right hand to carefully lift it out of the sling.

I explained to Jim that I was looking for unresolved emotions, and by using EFT we could release those emotions. If we were successful, we might see some kind of improvement in his condition. Grief seemed to be the most prominent emotion. Jim told me that during the first month after his stroke, he cried all the time. He admitted he had experienced a lot of loss, even before the stroke. Many people he was close to had "checked out" (his eyes glistened as he spoke of his friends who had passed on). Then there was the grief of being unable to use his body the way he had, and the many things that he couldn't do now.

Jim reported that his grief intensity level was a 5, but that in reality, if we dug a little, it was more like 10. The setup phrases we used were: Even though …

- I feel deep grief for all of the loss that I have had in my life, I deeply and completely love and accept myself.
- I feel grief over all of the friends that have checked out …
- I feel grief over not being able to use my body …

At first, I tried tapping on him, but then decided it would be best for him to tap on himself. It was difficult for him to tap on his karate chop point, so he began tapping it against the corner of a table.

During the first round, the reminder phrase was "deep sadness." Then I started feeding back the particular points he had brought up for a couple of rounds, repeating the ones that seemed strongest.

Then I asked him to rant about everything he was grieving about. Many of the things he included had to do with not being able to live on his ranch in the country, and missing his old life. His intensity level for his grief dropped to a 4/10. A couple more rounds of tapping brought it down to a 0, and he said he felt relaxed. The tension in his hand dropped from a 9 to 7 to 5.

Next we decided to work on his anxiety. His intensity level for anxiety was about an 8. He was anxious that he wouldn't get better, that he wouldn't be able to resume his active, ranch-based lifestyle. The anxiety intensity level dropped pretty quickly (2-3) with tapping, but then we started talking about his anxiety around falling, and his intensity level popped back up to a 5 before quickly dropping to 0. I looked at his hand and it appeared more relaxed. I asked him to consider the metaphor of his hand holding grief, and that today he had let go of some of it.

Then I asked him to walk, and since he wasn't feeling anxious about falling, he moved with much more confidence and balance than he had when I had first seen him. He was able to accomplish this with just two hours of releasing grief and anxiety using EFT.

Again, I am so impressed and grateful for what EFT can do.

22

Diabetic's Leg Swelling Disappears in 10 Minutes

TO HEAL FROM THE INSIDE OUT IS THE KEY.

~ Wynona Judd

Bill, my step-brother's father-in-law, is part of my extended family. Although 89 years old, he has always been quite active. He loves taking care of his exotic plants, which give his home the feeling of being in Hawaii (where they lived for several years). He also enjoys getting out and walking their two little dogs (a shitzu and a beautiful little stray) in the park.

My mother told me that Bill had recently fallen and fractured his pelvis, and that he also had to have some back surgery. His wife, Bettie, and my mom hadn't been able to go to the casinos since Bill had taken his fall, because Bettie had taken on more responsibility to care for him. Besides care giving, she had to do all the chores that Bill wasn't able to do, including grocery shopping – which she hated.

On the last day of a recent trip to visit my mother, we were able to see Bettie and Bill. We enjoyed the shade from his tropical plants as we chatted in their courtyard. After catching up, I told them about

EFT and how I thought it could benefit them. My mother didn't want to stay long so I explained how EFT worked quickly. Bettie had chronic pain in her knee that she said had an intensity level of 4. Bill was on all kinds of meds but he said that, at the moment, his back wasn't hurting. He showed us his swollen leg – I hadn't known he was diabetic. He mentioned that he had a doctor's appointment the next morning because of his leg.

We squeezed in one round of EFT. Both Bettie and Bill tapped with me for the first time. Bettie was astonished to find the pain in her knee had disappeared. Bill commented that his ankle felt less stiff.

The next morning, as I packed my suitcase to head home, my mother handed me the phone with a smile on her face. It was Bill. He said, "I think you are really onto something." He went on to tell me that the swelling had decreased in his legs and that they were much better – so much so that he cancelled his doctor's appointment.

I checked in with him several days later and the swelling was still down. He said that he was sold on tapping and had even done some on his own.

23

Fear of Water Shifts to Excitement in Five Minutes

FEAR IS EXCITEMENT WITHOUT BREATH.

~ Steve Ryals

Kamala, a sweet little three-year-old girl at the time of this story, happens to be my goddaughter. She has beautiful blue eyes just like her mother, Kristin. I had taken my granddaughter, Tessa, to meet with Kristin and Kamala at a toddler's swim class. After the class, we went into the hot tub, and then Kristin suggested that we all go play in the outside pool.

It was a gorgeous day and the outdoor pool felt deliciously warm. We happily shared the pool with a senior water exercise class, watching women rhythmically moving their bodies across the pool. Kristin and our little ones hung out near the steps in the shallow water.

Tessa and I played together, counting to three, before I threw her as high in the air as I could. When she splashed down, I followed her under water. With our eyes open and huge grins splashed across our faces, we swam up to the surface. Kristen tried to coax

Kamala out into the deeper water with us. Kamala, who was whining, didn't want to move off the step. Her mother kept saying, "Don't worry, Kamala, you will be safe."

I asked Kristin if it would be OK to do EFT with Kamala, and she nodded assent. Deciding that getting Kamala to tap probably wouldn't work, I chose to do some surrogate tapping (see Glossary). Looking into Kamala's eyes, I said, "Even though I am Kamala and I don't want to get all wet, I am an OK kid," and "Even though I am afraid of the water, I am an OK kid."

Kamala corrected me by saying that she didn't want to get her *face* wet. I added that to the setup phrase (while tapping on my karate chop points), "Even though I don't want to get my face wet, I am an OK kid." Then I started tapping the points on my body while I said reminder phrases such as: "Afraid of the water" and "Don't want to get my face wet." It only took one round and Kamala changed her stance. First she started laughing. Then all four of us were counting to three as Kristin and I tossed our little ones into the air. Kamala went under water and got her face wet, doing so without any fear. Kamala and Tessa kept screaming at the top of their lungs, "Again, again!"

In a few moments, my goddaughter had gone from terrified and whiny to delighted and excited. Once again, EFT came through.

24

Food Addiction Dissolves

JUST CAUSE YOU GOT THE MONKEY OFF YOUR BACK
DOESN'T MEAN THE CIRCUS HAS LEFT TOWN.

~ George Carlin

During the second class of my *I Love My Body* series (focused on losing weight) in the beautiful coastal village of Mendocino, CA, I told the group that those who were brave enough to work with me in front of the class would receive the greatest benefit. Those not willing to take a risk would miss out big time. When I asked for a volunteer, a woman named "Teresa" stepped forward. She confessed to feeling a lot of shame about sneaking around her house eating chocolates and then hiding the wrappers from her adult daughter.

What impressed me about Teresa was her willingness to trust both me and the EFT process. Even though this was her first class (she had missed the first one) and we had never met before, Teresa was ready to jump off the cliff of her fears. I used Borrowing Benefits (see Glossary), where everyone chose something related to their own food or body issues. Everyone tapped along, repeating what I was guided (by Spirit) to have Teresa say.

After the first round, Teresa dropped the intensity of the shame she felt from a 10 to a 6. Then she told me that she just couldn't understand why she was sneaking chocolate. She also said that there was a role-reversal with her daughter, where her daughter would shame her about her behavior. When I heard that I had an ah-ha. In the second round, the setup phrases I used addressed Teresa's inner child. They went something like this: Even though...

- I am not sure why I feel shame about sneaking chocolate, I deeply and completely love and accept myself.
- "Little Teresa" thinks it is fun to sneak around so my daughter, who is acting like my mom, doesn't see what I am doing ... *and* I forgive myself for playing this game.
- It is fun to sneak and pretend that I am getting away with something – even though I really am not – I know that I am sneaking chocolate – it has been a fun game ...

While we tapped, we called her daughter a bitch, and that helped her laugh at her situation. Remember, I always try to use humor to lighten up the situation. Teresa was both laughing and crying as she tapped, which brought her intensity down to a 0. Then someone offered her some candy, which she calmly refused. She felt as though a miracle had happened.

During the next class, she shared with the group that she had stopped sneaking around eating chocolate. Not only that, her daughter had noticed a positive difference in her energy. As she spoke, Teresa literally beamed, totally pleased with the shift in her behavior.

I wrote this article some time ago. When I saw Teresa recently, she confirmed that she was still not sneaking chocolate and had dropped one pant size, Way to go Teresa!

25

Relieving Marijuana Cravings

IT'S NEVER TOO LATE TO HEAL.
IT'S NEVER TOO LATE TO RESOLVE
UNFINISHED BUSINESS.
~ Alexandra Kennedy

"John" came to me because, though he views marijuana as a medicine and has been using it for much of his life, he wanted to drastically cut back on his use. I asked him what his goal was in terms of using marijuana, and he said that he would like to smoke it only on weekends and for creative endeavors.

He confessed that he felt as though he was addicted to pot. John said that he smoked it several times a day. He used marijuana to get in touch with his body. He smoked before he worked (he makes his living as a handyman); he uses it before he writes poetry; he smokes before he spins fire and works out.

After talking with John for a while, it seemed clear that he felt marijuana helped him to meditate, to breathe and to connect with his spirit. He liked the feeling of being a cool dude, and his inner teenager wasn't sure if he could be cool without pot.

He seemed to enjoy marijuana so much that I asked him why he wanted to cut back. He replied that he would soon be starting an inside job, and he wanted to be clean when he went to work. He also complained that his lungs hurt and in the morning he sometimes wheezed. John also complained about his penchant for getting speedy on strong coffee and then mellowing out with a joint, repeating the cycle several times a day.

I asked him if he had any marijuana on him, and he pulled out a small stash. I asked him to smell it, trying to get his craving to spike. The intensity was only a 3 or 4 out of 10. Since I hadn't known what the session would be about, I hadn't been able to ask him to refrain for the day, at least until after our session. Because he had smoked some pot a couple of hours before, I realized I had my work cut out for me.

His first set phrases were: Even though …

- I have been smoking marijuana most of my life, I deeply and completely love and accept myself.
- Marijuana helps me drop into my body …
- I don't know if I can go without marijuana for a day …

He tapped for several rounds and when he stopped I had him smell the pot and his craving went up to a 5-6. I asked if he had any insights, and he said that he really identified with marijuana.

During the next set of rounds we used "being cool" as a reminder phrase. After tapping, he smelled the marijuana again, and I had him imagine inhaling the smoke deeply into his lungs, then watching the smoke curl up, and then deeply feeling the immediate gratification of dropping into his inner self (these were all things he had told me). His intensity had gone up to an 8. Had I gone too far?

Was it getting close to the time when he would normally smoke his evening joint? When I asked him about it, he answered truthfully that it was.

Some of the final set-phrases we used included: Even though …

- My inner teenager wants to smoke pot whenever I want, there is another part of me that wants to be in control of this situation, and I deeply and completely love and accept myself, and I forgive myself for letting marijuana be in control of me.
- I am the Ganja King …
- I am not sure of who I will be without marijuana controlling me …

His reminder phrase was "Ganja King." After a couple of rounds I had him tap and bitch about his fears of life without weed.

After an hour and a half session, his intensity was still hovering around a 6, and he needed to be on his way. I told him that it looked as though we had more work to do.

The next morning he called to tell me that he had gone dancing and he did not smoke marijuana! He assured me that he felt fully in his body without it. Some time later I saw John in the market. He still had not used any herb since our session. Smiling from ear to ear, he thanked me profusely for my help.

26

Tailbone Pain Disappears

PAIN HAS MEANING AND A MESSAGE.
OUR EMOTIONS GIVE US VERY POWERFUL
FEEDBACK FOR AREAS WHERE WE NEED TO GROW.
~ *O. Carl Simonton, MD*

Almost every Thursday for well over two years, I took my young granddaughter to a toddler's swimming class. On one occasion, "Jenny," the swimming instructor, was not in the pool when we arrived. I found her standing next to the water, and she was still in her street clothes, which was really unusual. During the entire time I'd been taking Tessa to these classes, I had only seen Jenny out of the pool on one other occasion (when she had a bad cold).

When I inquired, I learned that Jenny had fallen down five days before, hurting her tailbone and her left hand in the process. She had taken some pain medication earlier in the day. I told her that if she would like to try some EFT with me, I thought I could help her feel better.

We met Jenny in an activity room of the health club. Jenny wasn't able to sit down because of her tailbone pain. We chatted while the kids climbed under the tables and hopped about as two and three-year-olds are inclined to do.

Jenny told me that the physical pain level right then was only about a 4/10. However, as she explained how she had fallen from a chair, and that her partner hadn't heard her calls, I could see how upset she was about his apparent lack of attention. She felt abandoned when he didn't come, and upset that he scolded her like a child (she is almost 70 years old) when he found out that she had fallen off a chair while trying to reach for something. She wanted to feel love from him. Instead, he had been acting like a mean father.

We tapped on the feelings that came up, including anger, frustration, and resentment towards her husband. She asked for so little in life, and she was angry (the intensity was an 8) that he wasn't able to give her empathy when she asked for it. I could see tears well up in the corners of her eyes, and we kept tapping to get it all out. When the intensity dropped to around a 5, I had her argue with herself while tapping, then affirm these positive statements:

- I want to let go of my anger, frustration, and resentment towards my husband, because these stuck emotions no longer serve me
- No, I don't, I want to be mad at him some more
- Yes, I do want to let this go
- No, I am not quite sure if I am ready to let this go
- I choose to let all of this go
- I am able to go to the calm place that is always within me
- I am whole and complete
- I experience the love that is always deep within me
- I feel relaxed and calm
- I am in balance

Before we knew it, we had chatted and tapped for about 25 minutes. She had never heard of EFT before our encounter. She sat down at the table. She hadn't been able to sit down for days, and she did it with ease. We cleared the emotional pain, and to her surprise the ache that she had felt where she had fallen on her tailbone had vanished.

A small miracle happened that day, though for Jenny it wasn't that small.

Here is a note that I got from her a week later.

Hi JoAnn,

Oh, WOW. The tapping and the issues I had when I was doing the work with you seem to have changed my being. I was very calm when I left the club. I stayed in my car for prayer time ;-)

Thank you so much,

Jenny

27

Poison Oak Miracle

EVENTUALLY YOU WILL COME TO UNDERSTAND THAT
LOVE HEALS EVERYTHING, AND LOVE IS ALL THERE IS.

~ Gary Zukav

Not long ago, my husband and I were in Santa Cruz visiting with
my daughter, Christina, and her partner, Liam. I was surprised
when Liam shared with a friend how he had witnessed me helping someone relieve their extreme poison oak rash. I had forgotten
that Liam had actually seen what had happened. My mouth was
hanging open when he described the poison oak rash disappearing
before his eyes.

Here's the story. Several years ago, not long after I started doing
EFT with other people, we were celebrating my birthday at my
sister-in-law's on the Smith River in far Northern California. It was
the beginning of autumn, and the leaves were turning beautiful
shades of yellow and gold. The poison oak had transformed into
several gorgeous shades of red, a truly wondrous sight.

Eileen, our hostess, had invited a good friend over. I wanted to
demonstrate the power of EFT to both Eileen and her friend, who

I'll call "Virginia." I decided to use Borrowing Benefits and work with two people at once. I don't remember what Eileen's issue was, but Virginia had a severe poison oak rash on the crease of her inner arm. It was bright red and oozed fluids.

We did a couple of rounds of EFT with both Eileen and Virginia tapping along. To everyone's amazement, Virginia's poison oak rash:

- Began to shrink
- Turned from bright red to pink
- Stopped oozing
- Didn't itch as much

I keep telling everyone to try EFT on everything. What do you have to lose? Maybe a miracle will happen. Are you ready for a miracle? You won't know if you don't tap.

28

Middle-Aged Student Passes Biology Class

BURNOUT IS NOT A CRISIS OF TIME SO
MUCH AS A CRISIS OF THE SPIRIT.

~ *James Autry*

I spent over two years as a co-moderator on the EFT Forum. On one occasion, a 57-year-old man posted a request for help with passing a class. Biology was the final class he needed to get his business degree. He had no interest in the class itself, and he was having a hard time connecting with his teacher's style. He wanted to be able to relax and get the best out of a class that he had put off until the end. He also wanted to be able to learn the material and pass the class – even though he was an older student who felt well past his prime.

Here is his post:

> Hi all: Here is my story. At 57 I'm taking my last gen. ed.
> class to graduate from business school. I have NO interest in
> Biology and our Prof. is not much of a teacher in a manner
> that brings about open discussions and questions. Rather,

we have a Power Point presentation, then she will ask if there are any questions. The students stare blankly while she just smiles. Later, we have a test on inter-cellular activity about which I have no clue. When I e-mail her questions, her answers are short and of little help.

My study papers are given the maximum points, the lab papers are given points within a 90% range, but on the tests the brain and body seem to have this inner sense of "justifying failure since everyone else is too." I want to excel!

So I want to learn how to tap so that I can relax and make the best of this class. I want to learn and pass the tests with a high degree of assurance, and to be able to answer them without sweaty hands and tension and successfully complete my course this December.

I work full time then go to school at night. I have been at this for over two and a half years. This is my last class. I've been told that I would never do much with my life, or that I was a loser. Years ago I asked for God's grace to allow me to live to my fullest potential regardless of the opinions of others. So I don't know if EFT works but I've read enough e-mails that I'm ready to try it.

I'll give my gratitude in advance for someone being kind enough to share their insight with me.

Thank You ...

Here's my response:

You have certainly come to the right place. Thank you so much for coming forward with your issue. Your willingness to work through it on the EFT Forum will no doubt help others as well. I will give you some ideas, and you can use those that seem the most helpful.

Here are some setup phrases for you to play with: Even though …

- I'm not sure if EFT really works, I deeply and completely love and accept myself.
- Some people may think that I'm too old to pull this off. I don't care about biology and our teacher isn't very good …
- I have a problem with our professor's teaching style …
- The professor isn't teaching to my learning style and she doesn't seem that interested in me passing this class …
- I was told that I would never do much with my life …
- They told me I was a loser …
- I'm letting the negative opinions of others affect me …
- I'm having a problem with completion …
- Part of me is afraid I can't do this …

Also, get in touch with the feelings you have with this whole situation. Connect with the core emotions that lie underneath your sweaty palms and chronic tension. These "hidden" emotions could include fear of failure, disappointment, anger at the professor or possibly anger at yourself for believing the negative (and false!) stories from your past.

After you clear some of these core issues, begin to affirm the truth of who you really are. I have found that if there is any *underlying* negative self-talk, even the clearest affirmations don't work as well. That is one of the reasons why EFT is so awesome! After getting rid of negative self-talk, be sure to affirm, "Yes, I can do this," (whatever "this" is). In your case, "Yes, I do deserve to finish this class and get my degree."

Please let me know how it turns out. Affirm that you can complete this biology class, even with the professor being just the way she is.

Almost two months later he wrote back:

Thank you! I will share that one night this past summer I woke up in a panic that I had failed a class and I saw the "F" on my grade. I managed to get back to sleep, realizing that I must have had a bad dream. Then, as soon as this class started, I got ill inside and "just knew" this was the class!

So this afternoon after a half dozen rounds, the word panic came to mind. I tapped until the pain under my arms subsided considerably! I was amazed. I will continue to perform EFT on this one topic until I know that this will be successfully completed. But, as with riding a bike, I'm on training wheels and appreciate the keen insight you showed.

I wrote him back right away. Here's what I said:

You are still passing–yay!

Just wondering, how do you feel about your dream? My recommendation is to get down to your feelings. If it were me (and I know it isn't) I would be feeling scared. I might say something like, "Even though I have test anxiety, I completely and wholly accept myself."

Yet for you, it doesn't seem to be going deep enough. Do you cuss? If you do, spice it up. **Get loud!** What happens if you fail your test? You want to get down to the nitty gritty – get away from the textbook-sounding phrases – you want to get down to your own self-talk. What are you telling yourself? Whatever the answer is becomes the basis for the setup phrases you will use to go all the way to the core of what's getting in the way of living the life of your dreams.

Here are some setup phrases that may work: Even though …

- I am scared sh**less that I am going to mess up on this test, and that if I do, I don't know how I will graduate, I deeply and completely love and accept myself.
- I hate this class, and no one can make me like it …
- I don't like it that I am the oldest person in class and I hope it isn't affecting my progress …

Sooooo, if these setup phrases don't work, send me the ones you are working with, and I will help you with them. Yes, say each setup phrase three times. Before you do that you want to figure out what the intensity is, 10 being the highest. When you are tapping, focus on your fears of failing the test. I find it is best to include a humorous reminder phrase, something along the lines of: "Stupid f**king test."

Personally, I don't start affirming the positive until the intensity gets down to at least a 3.

Here's his final post:

> Here's closure and an update. I passed my Biology class with a 'B.' I also used EFT to treat carpal tunnel pain along my whole arm from a bad ergonomic desk and computer use. WOW! It worked! The pain left before the third round. The Biology thing was strange. Somehow it just got a bit easier to grasp. The professor became less of an issue and I was able to help another lady that had really struggled with a positive attitude. I gave her lots of encouragement and helped her with her labs and test studies.

It felt good to give and share with others. I have to say that as much as I still doubt if it works, all I can say to new users is try it on everything, and yes it does work, even when it seems that nothing is happening!

"That's great news," I wrote back. "Woo-hoo!"

29

Releasing the Pain of a Son's Suicide

IT IS NOT DEATH THAT IS THE TRAGEDY OF LIFE.
IT IS WHAT YOU LET DIE WHEN YOU ARE ALIVE.
–Robert Muller

When I reach out to a friend in need, I don't always know whether what I have done has helped. Some time ago we visited with one of my husband's high school friends. "George's" bipolar teenage son had committed suicide eight years before by shooting himself in their family room. He died in George's arms.

We were vacationing with George and his wife at Big Bear. Even though I didn't know George very well, I could tell that he was walking around with a heavy heart. After we were together for a couple of days, I got up the nerve to ask him if he wanted to talk about his feelings surrounding his son's death.

With a blank face, he started telling me what had happened. He went into considerable detail, but it's not necessary to share all the particulars here. If it were a movie, I asked him, how long would it be, and what would be the title? After thinking about it for a minute, he replied, "Shock and Horror," and that it lasted two to three minutes.

When George imagined the movie of his son dying, he felt terror, panic, and helplessness. He reported that the intensity of his emotions in that moment was 3-4. He experienced these emotions manifesting as tightness in his chest.

After several rounds of tapping, I asked what was going on for him. George said he was re-living the pain of losing his son, and the intensity was still 3-4. We did another round, and the intensity went down to a 3, and he said he felt more relaxed. After two more rounds of tapping, he flashed back to turning his son over and seeing all the blood. He described the overwhelming shock and panic he felt. He recalled telling his wife to call 911. Having been trained as a medic in the Navy, he could see that his son was dying. He felt as though a lightning bolt had struck him.

George explained that ever since, at least once a day for the past eight years, he felt struck again by that lightning bolt, and it kept the memory of that terrible day alive. He said he feared forgetting the pain, that if he forgot the pain he might forget his son, and that the ongoing agony had become part of who he was. A few more rounds of tapping cleared the tightness in his chest, and brought the intensity down to 0.

Tonight my husband got a phone call from George, wishing him a happy birthday. It had been months since they'd talked, and almost a year and a half since I had worked with George. He told my husband how much he appreciated me taking the time to work with him, and that after our session the lightning bolt *never came back*. As I sat quietly, meditating on the miracle of EFT, I felt tears of gratitude trickling down my cheeks. I only wish that everyone who has experienced the loss of a loved one could find the peace that George has.

30

Help for a Minor Burn

NO EXPERIENCE IS ENERGY NEUTRAL. IT EITHER GIVES
YOU ENERGY, OR YOU LOSE A LITTLE ENERGY.

~ Rosalyn Bruyere

Wow, what a beautiful day in my garden! We'd had temperatures up in the 70s the past few days, and the plants were loving it. I was still getting tomatoes, which for mid-November up here in the mountains is truly amazing. We'd also had over 9" of rain already, so the hills were turning the most exquisite shade of green.

While strolling through the garden, I noticed a pile of debris that I had stacked during the summer. There were dried artichoke flowers, sunflower heads and stems, burdock stalks and seeds in the pile. Blackberry vines and various other things I didn't want to put in the compost were also stacked in this pile. There was just a slight breeze so I decided it would be a good day to burn.

After I started the fire, I used a pitchfork to toss material back into the center. The end of the pitchfork fell off (it was old, and the handle had rotted). I picked up some small pieces of burning material with my bare hands and threw them back onto the center of the fire. Can you guess what happened? I burned myself. I hadn't noticed that one of the pieces was red-hot where I grabbed it, and the palm of my hand instantly began to throb. I immediately decided to use EFT. I didn't bother giving a number for the intensity of the pain. I just started tapping on the karate chop point immediately, saying: Even though...

- It was really stupid for me to pick up that burning branch with my bare hand, I deeply and completely love and accept myself.
- It really hurt where I burnt my palm …
- I wish I wouldn't have been so stupid to pick up that burning branch with my bare hands …

In the first round of tapping, I enthusiastically used "really stupid" as my reminder phrase. My second, third and fourth rounds included ranting about how stupid I felt for picking up a hot branch with my bare hands.

Two hours after I burned my palm, I could still see a red mark. The intensity of the pain was down to about a 1. Five hours after the incident, the intensity was less than a half, and the red mark was barely visible.

So, how can you use this information? Let's say you get hurt somehow. You can ask yourself, "How do I feel about what just happened?" Many times when we get hurt we feel stupid or embarrassed. Get in touch with how you feel and start tapping.

(**NOTE:** Remember, if you have doubts about EFT working for you, use the following setup phrase three times before starting to tap about what happened: "Even though I doubt that EFT will work for me, I deeply and completely love and accept myself.")

When you're ready to start tapping on your immediate issue, begin with your setup phrase using this formula:

"Even though _____ (include how you feel. If you're struggling to identify your feelings, consult the "Feelings when Needs are not Fulfilled" chart in the Appendix), I deeply and completely love and accept myself." Repeat your setup phrase three times while tapping on the karate chop point on the side of your hand.

Then start tapping on the other points. You can use a reminder phrase to help you remember why you are tapping. Continue tapping and ranting about what just happened until you feel relief. If you feel embarrassed because people are watching you tap, you may choose to go somewhere private: outside, a bathroom, your bedroom, or your car. The important thing is to tap and release any emotions you may be feeling so you can speed up the healing process.

31

Releasing Math Anxiety

WHAT YOU CHOOSE NOT TO LOOK AT
IN YOUR LIFE RULES YOUR LIFE.

~ Lynn Andrews

One time I went on a house call. A woman named "Marsha" had asked me to work with her 10-year-old son, "Jimmy," who was having a hard time at school. During the intake, I learned that Jimmy was the oldest child, with two younger sisters.

At first, Marsha stayed in the room with us. She had done some EFT with a local therapist, and thought I might be able to help her son. Jimmy soon told me that he didn't like school. He hated wearing uniforms, and he didn't like to learn. He had just transferred from another school and was trying to understand 5th grade math even though he tested at the 2nd grade level. Jimmy added that he would do computer lab all day if he could, though he was just learning how to type.

We tapped on Jimmy's not liking math. Before we started, I told him that we were going to knock down his block to math, and that would make it easier. Some setup phrases included: Even though …

- I don't like math, I am an awesome kid.
- Math is my least favorite subject …
- I would rather take computers all day long, instead of having to take math …

He tapped on his karate chop point while vigorously repeating the setup phrases. Then, for the first round, I had him tap on the points on his body, saying "I don't like math." During the next round I had him say phrases such as, "I don't like math; I would rather play with computers all day; math has never been easy for me."

Then I asked Jimmy to close his eyes and notice how his block to math was now. He said that the strangest thing had happened, that his math wall had been as tall as the ceiling (the ceiling was about 12 feet high), and it was now only a couple of feet high. He closed his eyes, then told me that he had just smashed at the wall with a mallet, and then blew it up with five sticks of dynamite. I asked if he would be willing to go get his math book and do a problem. He read it to me, and then figured it out without any trouble.

Not long after this session with Jimmy, I received an e-mail from his mother. In it she wrote,

> *Things are going well with Jimmy. He seems to be getting his homework done with little resistance and we are excited about that. The proof will be after his first test. I have reminded him about the negative self-talk and tapping. We have developed a hand signal for when we are in a public place and I want him to tap to calm his anger. Works wonderful.*

Within 18 months, Jimmy had gone from three years below grade level to getting 80% scores in math at his grade level.

32

Prostate Pain and Urinary Problems

EFT IS EASY, EFFECTIVE, AND PRODUCES AMAZING RESULTS.
I THINK IT SHOULD BE TAUGHT IN ELEMENTARY SCHOOL.
~ Donna Eden

My husband and I were visiting some old friends of his (I had never met them). We spent the night at their country home. "Mark" (who was 57 at the time) went to bed early because of severe prostate pain. I told him about a technique called tapping that might be useful. I was interested to see if tapping could help him because I had never worked on a prostate issue before. With his enthusiastic agreement we tapped together for about an hour. I told Mark that in my experience, several things help make EFT work better:

- Rapport with the practitioner (we had established rapport during dinner)
- Willingness – he was incredibly willing for the pain not to be there
- Persistence
- Physical ways of changing energy: laughing, deeper breathing, crying, growling, yelling, cussing loudly

I asked Mark where exactly he was currently experiencing pain. He said that the tip of his penis hurt, and that at times it reached an intensity level of 8/10. Sometimes the pain went all the way to his prostate gland. On this evening it was a 5. He also told me that while his doctor had prescribed antibiotics, he was trying to stay away from them as much as possible and had been off of them for a while. Setup phrases included: Even though ...

- My penis sometimes hurts like hell, I deeply and completely love and accept myself.
- My penis has a burning sensation ...
- My penis really hurts ...

For emphasis, I had him yell the different phrases. Also, I had him tap certain points for a prolonged time. I worked hard to get him to laugh, and eventually he did. After one round his pain dropped to 0.

The next issue we worked on was difficulty emptying his bladder. On average, Mark had to get up five times during the night to pee, standing there for a long time before anything would come out. When it did begin to dribble, it really hurt, and he had begun tensing up in anticipation of the pain. Setup phrases: Even though ...

- It has been hard for me to pee ...
- Sometimes it only comes out in a dribble ...
- When the pee only dribbles out it makes me feel like an old man and I hate that ...
- Sometimes I pee like an old man ...

Reminder phrases: (I had him alternate)

- It only dribbles
- Pee comes out slowly

Setup phrases: Even though ...

- In the past couple of years, my pee has come out slowly, I deeply and completely love and accept myself *and* my penis.
- I forgive myself and my penis for anything that I may have done ...

Reminder phrases: (I had Mark alternate and spend some time imagining the positive images)

- Even though it may come out in a dribble ...
- And then again it may come out like a race horse ...
- And sometimes just a dribble ...
- I relax and let it flow like Niagara Falls ...
- And sometimes it's slow and I relax ...
- And let it flow like a fire hydrant ...
- I just let it flow and go easy on myself ...
- If I feel angry because it isn't flowing, I just let the anger flow easily out of my penis ...

I told him when he got up to go to the bathroom to turn the faucet on (an auditory reminder) and tap, then consciously breathe and use one of these visualizations:

- Peeing like a race horse
- Let it flow like Niagara Falls
- Flow like a fire hydrant

The next morning Mark reported that he had gotten up fewer times during the night. He also mentioned that he had found it easier to pee. His favorite part, though, was that he had been pain free all night.

While lingering over a delicious breakfast, I noticed that Mark was still anticipating the pain coming back whenever he stood up. His face contorted in a grimace, as if to prepare for the pain he imagined was coming. I brought this to his attention, and asked him to close his eyes and imagine himself as a vigorous 40-year-old man, breathing and standing up easily. Then we tapped.

Setup phrases: Even though …

- I have been tensing my body before I stand up, and that anticipating the pain has helped to intensify it …
- Tensing my body before standing up has intensified the pain, I didn't know any better …
- Now, before I stand up, I breathe slowly, relax and imagine that I am 40-years-old, and then stand up easily.

Reminder phrases (as usual at this stage, we alternated):

- Releasing fear of penis pain
- It's easy to stand
- Go away penis pain
- It's easy to stand up
- Releasing penis pain
- Go away penis pain
- I am aware of my relaxed body
- It is easy for me to stand up

After we finished, he was able to stand up without clenching up in anticipation of the pain. This one session helped Mark cope with the pain until his successful surgery several weeks later.

33

Tap 'n Bitch

THE LIMBIC EMOTIONAL SYSTEM IS INTIMATELY TIED IN
WITH THE IMMUNE SYSTEM, AND BEING ABLE TO
DEVELOP AND EXPRESS OUR EMOTIONS
ALLOWS US A HEALTHY LIFE.

—*Carla Hannaford*

Why carry around toxic emotional baggage? It simply isn't necessary. All you need is to remember to Tap 'n Bitch. If you take the time to use this process, you will not only have more energy, you'll feel great!

Tap 'n Bitch is a powerful technique. Any time you find yourself spinning your wheels about a certain situation, event, issue or circumstance, there is something dramatic you can do that is both easy and fun. We all know that toxic emotions stored in the body often turn into dis-ease. So why wait and let them turn into something nasty, when you can get it out now?

The first step is to decide on the issue. In other words, you need to be *specific*. **The second step** (though this step is optional, I highly recommend it) is to come up with a number between 1 and 10 that represents the intensity of your feelings about this issue, with 10 being the highest. You may want to write the number down so you can refer to it later.

I have so much fun with Tap 'n Bitch, and I think you will too. Start with your first point, and while tapping, bitch about your issue. Go ahead! Whine, complain, make pathetic excuses – really go for it! Continue for about 10 seconds or so on each point, then take a breath and move to the next, bitching all the way. Add lots of colorful words and cussing to spice up your bitching. This really helps move the energy, and that's the idea with EFT. You want to get the stuck energy out of your system.

After you've completed a round or two, check your intensity level and compare it with where you started. If you still feel a charge and you can't think of new things to say – repeat yourself! The goal is to get the intensity level as close to 0 as possible.

Please do not try Tap 'n Bitch while driving or operating heavy equipment. If you're shy, or care about what others think of you, I suggest not doing this in your local coffee shop or other public place. Find somewhere private (while stuck in traffic, say) and let it rip!

What makes this easier than regular EFT is that you don't have to come up with a setup phrase which, for many people, *especially* newbies, is the hardest part about EFT. With Tap 'n Bitch, you don't have to worry about making one up.

If you don't remember all of the points, that's OK. Just tap on the ones you do. Remember Joe from chapter 15? He was able to use Tap 'n Bitch even though he could only remember one point. His intent was so strong that it still worked.

Tap along with my Tap 'n Bitch video at http://bit.ly/FSuAy

34

Clearing the Pain of a Rocky Economy

OUR RESPONSE TO AN EVENT IS MORE
IMPORTANT THAN THE EVENT ITSELF.
– Angeles Arrien

Do you have a physical symptom that coincides with a loss? Perhaps you have recently lost your job, house, relationship or health insurance. If you have "coincidentally" noticed a "new" physical problem, they may actually be connected. With people losing their jobs and even their homes, the last few years have been a time of uncertainty. EFT can be a powerful tool for these fractious times where we may not always know where to turn.

In my opinion, what is important is to get to the root cause that lies buried underneath any particular condition. For example, I was commenting on a post made in the EFT Forum on Pain. The topic of the post was: "Unknown symptom and cause."

This person had an earache. I suggested that he should go deeper than the problem with his ear. Here are some setup phrases I suggested: Even though …

- I don't know what is causing this problem with my ear, I deeply and completely love and accept myself.
- My ear may be trying to tell me something, and I don't know if I am ready to hear what it is ...
- I am in sales and I am not able to pay my bills, and I don't know what to do ...
- My body is trying to give me a clue, and I'm not sure what it is ...

I suggested that before you start tapping, rate the ringing and numbness so you know where you are starting (this is an important step, and one that I forgot to do many times when I was first getting started). Then say the above phrases while tapping on the side of your hand. Then, when you tap on your body points, use something such as, "this ear symptom," as a reminder phrase. Continue tapping and ranting in order to get it all out:

- I don't have any insurance
- My life is not in balance
- I can't pay the bills
- I don't know what I am going to do

Keep going until you get everything out – all of your deepest fears and whatever else is stuck inside you. Finally, when there is nothing left, stop tapping and ask yourself, "What is the message that my ear has been trying to tell me?" Listen. Check the ringing and numbness in your ears. Consider whether there might be someone (or something) in your life that you aren't listening to.

When the intensity gets down to a 3 or less, start affirming:

- I am whole and complete
- I am connected to my higher self (or whatever you call it)

- Things are working out
- When I get scared, I breathe into my fear and relax

So, if you have just lost your health insurance, a job, your house, or perhaps even your relationship, and you have noticed a "new" physical problem, they may well be connected. Tap on your feelings of loss and get it all out. Then check in with the intensity level of your physical symptoms. You may be surprised to find that they have lessened.

35

Tapping Back into Exercise

MOVEMENT IS A MEDICINE FOR CREATING CHANGE IN A
PERSON'S PHYSICAL, EMOTIONAL, AND MENTAL STATES.
~ *Carol Welch*

A client asked me how to use EFT to exercise. "Debbie's" life is very sedentary. She works 12-15 hours a day on her computer. Her resistance to doing exercise was 10/10.

Here are some of the setup phrases she used: Even though…

- I hate to exercise, I deeply and completely love and accept myself, and I forgive myself for not exercising very much these last couple of years.
- I am physically lazy …
- I am not a physical athlete, but I am a mental athlete, and I wish that I could think about exercising …
- My exercise has been to walk from the studio to the kitchen to the bedroom …
- There are not quite enough hours in the day …
- I have other things that I would rather do and need to do than exercise …

- There needs to be another one of me to do all of the things that I need to do ...

Debbie's reminder phrase was, "Resistance to Exercise." After four rounds of tapping, the intensity of her resistance to exercise came down to a 5. Then she admitted that she'd rather exercise than tap. You can probably guess her next setup phrase, "Even though I'd rather exercise than tap ..." and, "Even though part of me doesn't feel like exercising ..." When I sensed that the intensity had lessened even further, I had Debbie begin to affirm the positive:

- Exercising makes me feel wonderful
- I love the endorphins that flood my body when I exercise
- I love moving my body
- I love the way that exercise clears my mind
- Exercising makes me feel more energetic
- I feel calm and centered
- I have more than enough time to exercise

This brought her resistance to exercising down to a 1-1½. She shared with me that she felt like getting up and exercising right then, instead of waiting until the next morning. I enthusiastically encouraged her to do just that.

When I checked in with Debbie the next day, she related how she had gone out after our session and followed my advice about taking it easy. After a wonderful walk, she'd fallen asleep at 10 p.m. – unusual for her. She had gone for another walk just before we spoke.

Debbie wanted to know if she needed to continue tapping to help her exercise. My suggestion was to tap every time she didn't feel like exercising. If there was no resistance, then she wouldn't need to tap – just go out and walk!

36

Clearing a Food Aversion

IT'S NEVER TOO LATE TO HEAL. IT'S NEVER TOO
LATE TO RESOLVE UNFINISHED BUSINESS.
~ Alexandra Kennedy

On a hot summer morning, my husband, Steve, offered me some ripe, ice-cold cantaloupe. He said, "I know you have never cared for cantaloupe, but you might want to reconsider. It doesn't get any better than this." He smacked his lips for emphasis. I remembered hearing about people clearing food issues with EFT, so I agreed to give it a try. I had detested eating cantaloupe my whole life. My sister never like it either, which made me think that "something" had happened around cantaloupe when we were girls.

The setup phrases I used (while tapping on my karate chop point) were: Even though …

- I don't like the taste of cantaloupe, and I don't know why, I deeply and completely love and accept myself.
- My sister and I never liked the taste of cantaloupe …
- Something may have happened while we were eating cantaloupe, and I don't remember what it was …

Then I did a round of tapping. For the reminder phrases, I used:

- Don't like cantaloupe
- Doesn't taste good
- Don't like the taste
- Don't ever remember liking the taste

Then I took a taste. It was cold, somewhat crisp, and felt good in my mouth. It didn't taste quite as bad as I thought it would, but I couldn't say that I liked it. So, I did some more setup phrases while tapping on my karate chop point. Even though ...

- Cantaloupe has always tasted yucky to me ...
- Something happened to sour me on the taste of cantaloupe, and I don't remember what it was ...
- There is something about the aftertaste of cantaloupe I don't like ...

I did a round of tapping using the following reminder phrases:

- Yucky taste
- Yucky cantaloupe aftertaste

To test the effectiveness of my EFT session, I took a big bite of cantaloupe. "Yum, not bad," I said as I continued munching on it.

Within about ten minutes, I cleared a food aversion that I had carried around for over 50 years. Even though I had a sense that something may have happened in my past while I was eating cantaloupe, and even though I couldn't remember exactly what it was, I was still able to clear my resistance to the taste. Now, I can finally enjoy a food that I had eliminated from my diet when I was a child.

37

Healing a Guilty Conscience

HEALING MAY NOT BE SO MUCH ABOUT GETTING BETTER,
AS ABOUT LETTING GO OF EVERYTHING THAT ISN'T YOU —
ALL OF THE EXPECTATIONS, ALL OF THE BELIEFS —
AND BECOMING WHO YOU ARE.

~ Rachel Naomi Remen, MD

I really love tapping with groups. What Gary Craig calls "Borrowing Benefits," I like to call "Tuning into the One Heart." On my first Transformation Cruise, I did a 90 minute workshop called "Attracting Miracles." During the first part, I talked about Spirit and Essence. Then I led some exercises to help participants get in touch first with their essence and then with the essence of others in the room.

This story comes from watching the video of my workshop. I worked with three volunteers separately within a 40-minute period. The first two clients both had family members who had committed suicide. I quickly helped them clear their feelings around that hugely intense issue.

I believe that these long-standing hurts cleared quickly for several reasons. First, we were on a Law of Attraction Cruise, and our focus was on attracting the positive. Second, we had been focusing on how everyone is a miracle. Third, we were joining together and tapping into the power of the One Heart. It may sound woo-woo, but there truly is a power when people join together in Spirit.

As you've probably guessed by now, one of my favorite ways to work with EFT is by using humor. It helps make whatever condition the person is dealing with seem less overwhelming. They are able to see a different perspective. One way to create humor is by cussing (unless, of course, the person is totally against it).

Janice wanted to let go of the guilt she had been carrying around for two years, ever since her mother-in-law, Alice, had died. Janice's problem was that she had actually *wished* her mother-in-law would die, and then felt horribly guilty when she did. I asked Janice why she had wished her mother-in-law's death, and she replied, "Because she was a vicious, mean and hateful person who told a lot of lies."

I told the group that it doesn't really matter how long a person has had a problem, as long as they are willing to let go of playing the victim. Some people aren't willing or ready to let go of the victim role because there is a hidden payoff. Perhaps they identify with bring a victim so strongly that they don't know who they would be if they surrendered that role. They may even have an inner voice saying something to the effect of, "I'm a victim, therefore I am." The point is to let go of the victim role and become a survivor – "Survive and thrive" as I like to put it.

Janice was feeling so guilty about wishing for her mother-in-law's death that her intensity level was an 8. When I asked where she felt the guilt in her body, she said it was in her neck and that the intensity was a 4. Everyone repeated these long set-phrases while tapping on their karate chop points. Even though …

- I'm not sure if I can let this guilt go. I wished that Alice was dead and she died. It must be my fault because my intention was that strong. I made her die *and* I deeply and completely love and accept myself.
- I wished Alice would drop dead … and she did. I felt guilty ever since. I love that part of me that feels like it is my fault.
- I wished that Alice would die and she did. I've been carrying this guilt around and I forgive myself. She was mean. I couldn't help myself. I love and accept that part of me.

Then we all tapped on our meridians, inhaling and exhaling after each reminder phrase.

IE: Mean bitch
OE: Mean bitch
UE: She was a mean bitch
UN: I thought it was my fault that she died
UL: She was so mean
CB: I wasn't the only one that wished she was dead. I guess it was all of our minds working together
UA: Mean bitch
LP: Mean bitch (Janice was laughing)
TH: Mean bitch

After the first round of tapping, I asked Janice to close her eyes and go inside to notice any insights. She answered laughingly, "A lot of relief." Her guilt went from an 8 to a 3 and her shoulder pain went from a 4 to a 1. We did more setup phrases with everyone following along on their karate chop points. Even though …

- Alice was a mean bitch, she was doing the best she could. She had problems and she didn't know how to do any better. I love and accept myself for wishing she would die.

- I was doing the best I could do then. I didn't know any better. It gave me a sense of power when I wished she would die, so much so that I actually felt guilty when she did pass away, as though it was my fault. I choose to let this guilt go. I know that Alice died because it was her time. It wasn't me. It was Alice. I love and forgive myself.

I paused and asked what her intensity was around the guilt she had been feeling. It went from a 3 to a 2. Then we used these reminder phrases while tapping on our meridians.

IE: I forgive myself for wishing Alice were dead
OE: No, I don't. It was my fault
UE: Yes, I do
UN: No, I don't. I want to carry this around forever
UL: Yes, I do
CB: I choose to let this go
UA: I choose to let Alice be where she's at
LP: I forgive myself
TH: I am Whole and Complete

Someone in the audience added, "I forgive Alice," and we all repeated, "I forgive Alice."

Janice said that her guilt was gone and her shoulder pain was down to a 1. All of this happened in 13 minutes while tapping and tuning into the One Heart. Another miracle!

38

Heidi

HOWEVER GOOD OR BAD YOU FEEL ABOUT YOUR
RELATIONSHIP, THE PERSON YOU ARE WITH AT THIS
MOMENT IS THE "RIGHT" PERSON, BECAUSE HE OR
SHE IS THE MIRROR OF WHO YOU ARE INSIDE.

- Deepak Chopra

One day I had a phone session with a woman from Europe. "Heidi" told me that she would love to be in relationship with a man. It had been 10 years since she'd had a partner. Heidi related how she thought that she must be ambivalent about being with with someone. She realized that part of her would rather be alone, while another part would love to be in relationship.

Heidi recognized that the possibility existed for her to connect with a man who would not only meet her criteria, but would also want to spend time with her. She reported feeling little faith that such a man, assuming he existed, would be living in her area, and that if he did, she doubted that they would ever meet. In fact, Heidi had become convinced that the probability of ever meeting such a man was slim indeed. Now that she was older, in her late sixties, there weren't as many available men.

We examined what the payoff might be for remaining single, and she immediately replied that independence was one. She could do what she wanted whenever she wanted. She didn't have to clear her plans with anyone.

After thinking about the payoff of independence, Heidi decided that she would be willing to make the trade-off in order to be in a fulfilling relationship. She was tired of feeling lonely. She really wanted to have someone with whom to share her daily life. However, she was afraid of being dependent.

We looked at the relationship that she'd had with "James" 10 years previously, and she realized that she had lost her identity when she had become the "sacrificing" wife. One of her stories was that she was supposed to be a really good wife, and that she was responsible for her man's happiness. She was supposed to cook a nice meal, and get his clothes in order. Part of her loved being a good wife, and another part (her inner teenager) felt rebellious about being his maid, and not feeling equal.

She realized that she liked being a caretaker, but didn't like it when she wasn't appreciated. Heidi felt as though she had some bitterness towards James and that she had done a lot of sacrificing for him. The intensity of her feelings of sacrificing for James was a 7/10.

I asked her if James was just a trigger for her unresolved feelings of sacrificing her true self in order to be in relationship. Heidi shared that her mother had gotten pregnant with her on her honeymoon. Heidi was born small and felt unwanted even in the womb. She felt as though her sacrificing began in the womb. Her core wound was that everyone else's needs were more important than her own. Sacrificing for others became a lifelong mantra.

The intensity that Heidi felt about sacrificing in the womb was a 9, whereas the intensity of sacrificing for James was a 7. The experience with James was a trigger, so I had her tap on her in-the-womb experience of sacrificing. I asked her to come up with a reminder phrase that would make her laugh at the cosmic joke as well as making a crack in the cosmic egg. Her reminder phrase was "bunch of baloney."

After one round using the reminder phrase, "bunch of baloney," we were able to collapse the intensity to a 0. We were able to do all of this in around an hour. She then told me she hoped to invite me to her wedding in the future.

Here's her testimonial:

> *I found JoAnn "by chance" on www.Emofree.com and booked three sessions with her. What an absolutely wonderful experience! JoAnn helped me to find the deepest layers of my issues – and I found her use of combining the various feelings around an issue into one word as the essence – and also seeing my issue as a "cosmic joke" absolutely brilliant. I went from a 10, with an issue that started even prenatally, to a flat 0 within a few minutes!*

> *I recommend JoAnn without hesitation; nay, wholeheartedly!*

39

Bringing a Man into Her Life

HANG AROUND WITH PEOPLE THAT MAKE YOU LAUGH.
FIND OUT WHAT MAKES YOU LAUGH, AND START
GETTING MORE OF THAT IN YOUR LIFE.

– Allen Klein

I had worked with "Martha" before, helping her clear her mother issues. The other day we worked on clearing her old fear-based stories that seemed to be keeping the perfect guy away from her.

We spent an hour tapping away old stories and beliefs about men. I also used Lindsay Kenny's incredibly powerful "Ultimate Truth Statement" (UTS). With the UTS, you make a concise statement of what you want in the present tense. Include words about how you will feel when you get what you want.

Start by saying your UTS out loud. Determine the intensity of it in this moment. **Caution:** The rating system is the *opposite* of what we use with EFT. A 10 would mean that it feels really true. A 0 means that it feels absolutely impossible. If your intensity with the UTS is less than a 10, you work on letting go of the beliefs, stories and experiences that get in the way of you vibrationally experiencing what you want in your life. Then you use EFT to clear the resistance to what you want.

Martha's UTS was: "I am happily in relationship with a man in my area. Our relationship is based on mutual respect and love. We have lots of fun playing together."

We cleared all the stuff that came up, such as:

- I had crappy programming when I was a child, and I deeply and completely love and accept myself.
- My mother said, "You should never get married" …
- I'm a "runner" …
- I'm afraid of being left and made to feel stupid …
- I'm never good enough …
- There isn't a good guy in my town …
- I'm afraid of not being accepted …
- I don't feel safe …

We cleared everything that came up. The anxiety that she had been feeling in her stomach disappeared. She could say her UTS, "I am happily in relationship with a man in my area. Our relationship is based on mutual respect and love. We have lots of fun playing together," with absolute conviction. I suggested that she tape her UTS on her mirror so she could be reminded of it several times a day.

I'd also like to say that we did this work entirely over the phone. I have not met Martha face-to-face, and have no clue as to her appearance. I understand that she is on disability. The truth is, it doesn't matter. I bring this up to emphasize that healing old emotional trauma is an inside job. The physical package is irrelevant.

At the end of our hour together, Martha told me that EFT is her cup of tea, and that I am her teapot. She thought that was kind of funny because she doesn't even drink tea. I felt honored that she trusted me so much.

I received an e-mail from Martha a few weeks later. This is the essence of her communication:

Wow, here we are again. I met a neat man that I can play with. He lives in my area, and is into all the "way-out" spiritual stuff that I have a strong interest in. He has been on the internet and we have winked at each other for more than a year, and he finally gave me a way to contact him and I got gutsy and did. We talked for five hours last night ... he has what I like in the way of looks, a nice bad-boy type. His life has followed similar ways as mine ... will keep you posted you miracle worker. There are a few more men writing to me who also live in this area.

Thank you,

"Martha"

40

Failure Feelings Fade

ALL CHANGES, EVEN THE MOST LONGED FOR,
HAVE THEIR MELANCHOLY; FOR WHAT WE LEAVE
BEHIND US IS A PART OF OURSELVES;
WE MUST DIE TO ONE LIFE BEFORE
WE CAN ENTER ANOTHER.

~ Viktor Frankl

"Mariah" had been putting on events for decades. She gave me a call asking for a telephone session to help her sort through some issues around an important upcoming conference. The workshop leaders, as well as Mariah, were supposed to be registering people to attend the event (after first inviting and enrolling them, of course). At the time of our session, few of the leaders had registered anyone. Mariah was concerned that not enough people would sign up for the event to be a financial success.

I asked Mariah to come up with an Ultimate Truth Statement (UTS) in which she claims (in the present tense) what she would like. She came up with, "The event is successful on all levels, with at least 80 participants." Remember, when you use an Ultimate Truth Statement, it is rated differently than EFT. 10 is the perfect score, and 0 would mean you felt it was impossible. Mariah rated her Ultimate Truth Statement at a 4. Then I asked why her UTS was so low. She had lots of reasons, including:

- The state of California was in a depression
- There were hardly any sign ups and she had made most of them herself
- She was sad that it wasn't easier for workshop leaders to sign up participants
- She wasn't convinced that the potential participants were seeing the value of the conference
- She was worried that she chose the wrong date to have the event
- She was also concerned that she had scheduled this event too close to the last one
- She felt that it was all her fault

Mariah clearly felt like a failure. I asked her if the way she felt reminded her of anything from her past. She chuckled and explained that she had organized lots of events over the years, and most of them went well. However, there had been one years ago that didn't work, and she had been blamed.

I asked her to think about the failure of that conference and being blaming, and to notice if she still harbored any feelings about it. She was surprised to realize just how strong her feelings remained. In fact, a number 10 feeling of failure thundered in her stomach. She said it felt yucky. After one round of tapping, her sense of failure and being blamed dropped to a 5. I had her repeat her UTS, "The event is successful on all levels with at least 80 participants," and she said that it had gone from a 4 up to an 8. I could hear the growing enthusiasm in her voice.

She could see how she had been feeling like a victim again, just like she had years ago. They blamed her and she was blaming them. She felt as though they did nothing, that they wanted her to do it all. It was deja vu all over again.

Then she realized she was still angry about what had transpired years ago. She felt the anger in her stomach, chest and throat catch fire. She was amazed that it was an 8, even after all these years. She did one round of tapping on her anger for being blamed and not taking responsibility. After just one round of venting, she said the anger had disappeared.

Mariah then had the realization that even though others had thought the event was a failure, for the people who did attend, it was a great success. The same would be true for the upcoming conference. We went back to the feeling of failure she felt in her stomach. We did one more round of tapping about feeling blamed, about her blaming them and about others putting the responsibility on her, which brought the feeling of failure in her stomach from 5 to 0.

I asked her to repeat her UTS again, and this time it went from an 8 to a 10. Mariah now felt as though the upcoming festival would be a success, that the people who were supposed to show up would, and that they would get tons of value from it. In less than 45 minutes, Mariah was able to let go of her stuck feelings about the event that had flopped. She left the session with a new sense of determination that she would be able to do what was necessary to make the upcoming conference a success.

41

Ginger the Scaredy-Cat

WHEN I PLAY WITH MY CAT, HOW DO I KNOW THAT
SHE IS NOT PASSING TIME WITH ME
RATHER THAN I WITH HER?

~ Montaigne

Ginger is a sweet cat even though she's always been a scaredy-cat. Her mother was (mostly) feral and taught Ginger to be afraid of humans. Ginger's mother disappeared a few years ago, most likely munched by a bobcat that had been hanging out near our pond. We've had Ginger for four years, and she's a hardy outside cat who ruthlessly keeps down the mice population in our home. (Hey, what do you expect? She's a cat!)

Even though we feed Ginger, and she loves being petted (though only by us), she has never liked us picking her up or putting her on our laps. She has become a lot friendlier in the years since her mother vanished, and now sleeps on our bed most nights.

Just the other day, I really wanted Ginger on my lap. I was outside sitting in a lawn chair, and Ginger walked over to me. I tried picking her up but she immediately jumped out of my hands. So, I thought

I would try Surrogate EFT (see Glossary), on her. I didn't even have to physically tap on my cat. She's way too skittish for that.

Here is how I did it. I imagined that I was Ginger. I tapped on my karate chop point saying, Even though …

- My mother taught me not to trust people, I'm an OK cat.
- I've been afraid of people, including JoAnn, …
- I'm a scaredy-cat, and my mother taught me to be leery of people, …

I tapped on my meridians for one round, saying "scaredy-cat" as a reminder phrase.

Then I did another round, saying things such as:

- My mom taught me not to trust people
- Maybe I can trust JoAnn, she's been feeding me for my whole life
- JoAnn hasn't hurt me
- Maybe I can trust her
- Maybe it's okay for me to get on her lap
- I can trust JoAnn
- It's OK for me to get on her lap
- I feel safe on JoAnn's lap

After I finished, Ginger let me pick her up. She didn't struggle at all. I put her on my lap and didn't feel any resistance. I started to pet her and she let me. She stayed on my lap for 10 minutes, purring as I gently stroked her fur.

EFT is an amazing tool! Gary Craig says try it on everything, and that includes a scaredy-cat named Ginger.

42

I Didn't Think I Could Write

IT TAKES A LOT OF COURAGE TO RELEASE THE FAMILIAR
AND SEEMINGLY SECURE, TO EMBRACE THE NEW.
BUT THERE IS NO REAL SECURITY IN WHAT IS NO
LONGER MEANINGFUL. THERE IS MORE SECURITY IN
THE ADVENTUROUS AND EXCITING, FOR IN MOVEMENT
THERE IS LIFE, AND IN CHANGE THERE IS POWER.

~ Alan Cohen

Even though I have never seen myself as a good writer, I have used EFT to help me write and submit numerous articles on the internet. It's ironic, because my husband is an English graduate from UC Berkeley and has long been a writer and editor. After I started writing articles on EFT (which he happily edited), he often encouraged me to think about writing a book. Even with EFT, it took some time for me to jump off the cliff of my fears and start the book you now hold in your hands.

When I was a child, I hated grammar. When my mother would correct me, I resisted, and continued to use poor grammar – it became part of my identity. Part of my problem was that I never did well in English classes. I was a PE major in college, and when it was time to take an English class, I was able to take poetry writing instead of a regular writing class, which I was terrified of taking and possibly failing.

A little over 20 years ago, I was telling an inspirational story to a friend who had a local weekly newspaper. She encouraged me to write a column. I agreed to give it a try, and decided to call it *Minders*. I wrote about people successfully useing affirmations to better their lives.

The genesis of *Touched by a Miracle* was born out of the notes I took about my client's progress when we did EFT. It wasn't long before I started submitting healing stories to Gary Craig's *Insights Newsletter*. (Note: while no longer being published, the newsletter archives are still available at www.emofree.com/archives.aspx.) At first, I was surprised when my articles were published.

Let me back up and tell you what I did to get the confidence to write and submit stories in the first place. As I said, I just didn't see myself as a writer. A writer was someone totally different than me (or so my story went). Here are some of the setup phrases I used to let go of my old beliefs: Even though …

- I don't see myself as a writer
- I hated grammar as a child
- I resisted learning proper grammar as a child just to piss off my mother
- I got off on using poor grammar
- I didn't do that well in English classes as a youngster
- I don't have a good vocabulary
- I wrote a weekly newspaper column over 20 years ago, I still don't see myself as a writer
- A writer is someone different (smarter, better) than me

My husband, Steve Ryals, published *Drunk with Wonder: Awakening to the God Within*, in 2006. He told me repeatedly that I was a writer, which would always blow my mind. He also said that most writers have editors and, if I was patient, he'd be delighted to edit what I wrote, including this book.

Now I'm a writer, and it's difficult to even remember when I felt as though I couldn't write. The more I write, the easier it gets to put down my thoughts and communicate in ways that I never imagined possible. All I had to do was let go of my old "can't write" story and replace it with "I am a successful writer." As you must realize by now, EFT made the difference for me, just as it can for you, no matter what's going on (or not) in your life.

43

Boris the Spider

HEALING IS THE MOST NATURAL THING IN THE WORLD.
WHEN WE EMBRACE LIFE, WE ARE HEALED.

~ Richard Moss, M.D.

My nephew, Daniel, is quite knowledgeable about reptiles and arachnids. Ever since he was a little boy, when my husband, Steve, taught him how to be really still and catch a lizard, he has been quite fearless with snakes and spiders.

One time, Daniel had a big scare with a giant spider. He had been in a pet store holding a large tarantula (let's call it Boris) in a plastic container. He wanted to see what would happen if he blew on the spider's butt. Well, to his surprise, the tarantula moved in a way that scared him. Even though the Tarantula was in a plastic container, the unpredictable way in which the spider moved touched a primal dread and really terrified him.

I asked Daniel to close his eyes and imagine holding Boris in the plastic container and feeling the fear when the spider moved. I asked him to get in touch with the level of fear he was feeling in that moment, and he said his intensity level was a 7/10.

The setup phrases we used included: Even though I …

- Am knowledgeable about spiders, I still got scared by a spider, and I deeply and completely love and accept myself.
- Felt like running …
- Got really scared of that spider …

After a few rounds of tapping we got his intensity level down to a 3. I asked him a few more questions and discovered that he felt the strength of the spider when it moved, and that was what had scared him. He realized that it wasn't a wise idea to blow on the tarantula's ass – that at the very least it wasn't respectful.

So, he tapped while alternating statements such as:

- The strength of the spider really scared and surprised me
- It wasn't a good idea to blow on a tarantula's ass
- Next time I'll be more respectful of a spider

This brought his emotional intensity level down to 0. The next time I saw Daniel, several months later, he said that he didn't feel scared of spiders, and that when he thought of them he felt calm. Still, he made sure I knew that he hadn't blown on any tarantula butts lately.

44

Boy Develops "Air Tapping"

THE ART OF HEALING COMES FROM NATURE,
NOT FROM THE PHYSICIAN. THEREFORE THE
PHYSICIAN MUST START FROM NATURE,
WITH AN OPEN MIND.
~ *Philipus Aureolus Paracelsus*

I first met "Jimmy," when he was in the fifth grade (see chapter 31). When he was younger, he had been diagnosed with autism, but had thankfully outgrown his diagnosis. Eighteen months after our first session, his mother called me to see if I could help Jimmy with his anger issues.

The kids would pick on Jimmy, calling him names and making fun of him. Since Jimmy didn't want to get in trouble, when he got angry he would take it out on himself with nasty self-talk.

It had been quite a while since our previous session, so Jimmy was a little shy about working with me. During the first part of our session we just talked about his life. After we redeveloped a connection, I asked him about the kids at school making fun of him. He admitted that he felt pretty flustered with their name-calling.

I asked if he would like to know a way in which he could soothe himself when they picked on him. He told me he would like that very much.

I showed him the basics of tapping, and had him do a couple of rounds to release some of the anger. He didn't relate to using numbers for the intensity of his emotions, but he did relate to opening his arms all the way for the highest intensity, and putting his hands together for 0 intensity. Instead of using, "I deeply and completely love and accept myself," for the last part of the setup phrase, I simply had him say, "I am an awesome kid." We were able to collapse his anger in a couple of rounds.

I asked Jimmy if he had any favorite tapping points, and he replied that he had three. I explained that these are called "sweet spots" and that he could ignore the other points. One of his sweet spots was his karate chop point. I showed him how he could hold his karate chop point so that other people wouldn't even notice when he chose to use it, and also how he could nonchalantly (and discreetly) press his other sweet spots when he needed to use them. He really liked this concept.

NOTE: An effective alternative to tapping on points, especially in a public environment when discretion seems warranted, is to lightly rub or press on the point - no actual tapping required. I urge you to experiment. Remember, you can't do it wrong.

Quite interestingly, since our first session Jimmy had developed his own method of tapping. He called it "air tapping." When he needed to self-soothe, he would tap his sweet spots *in his imagination*. He was able to tap successfully with no one even aware of what he was doing. I thought this was brilliant, and told him so. His smile lit up the room!

45

Putting Worry on a Shelf

WORRY NEVER ROBS TOMORROW OF ITS SORROW,
IT ONLY SAPS TODAY OF ITS JOY.

~ Leo Buscaglia

I could hear "Sara's" exhaustion in her voice. The past couple of weeks had tuckered her out. She had taken a 12 hour train ride to visit her mother and sister for a week. On her return trip, the train was an hour late, arriving after midnight. Her son, excited to see her, wanted to talk until 2:30 a.m., which was well past her bedtime. The next thing she knew, her three-month-old grandson woke her up at 5 a.m.

When Sara finally returned home after five more hours in the car, she had classes to teach and presentations to prepare. She felt as though she didn't have enough time to do everything that needed to be done, and that she was working her fingers to the bone.

We did several rounds of EFT on Sara's exhaustion, yet her intensity level dropped only from a 7 to a 5.5. My intuition told me to ask more about her visit to her invalid mother, and I found that underneath her tiredness bubbled great worry. Sara was deeply concerned about the care that her mother was getting from Sara's sister. Sara was also worried that her sister, who she described as irrational, was going to freak out while taking care of their mother. Living so far away didn't help, because there was no easy way to verify what her sister was telling her.

I asked Sara to put a number on the intensity level of her worrying about her mother's care, and when she said that it was 9.5, I knew that worrying was taking a lot of her energy. It was easy to see how her worry could very well be making her tired. We did a few rounds focusing on how much she was worrying, which brought her intensity level to a 2. Another couple of rounds brought it to a 0. Coincidentally, her tiredness went from a 5.5 to a 2 before dropping to 0 as well.

Sara really liked the idea I gave her about putting her worry on a shelf. After all, she could pick it up and dust it off again any time she wanted. After doing our EFT session, she said that she still felt tired, but that it was a normal, healthy, tired feeling and that she had let go of feeling utterly exhausted.

I saw Sara the next day, and she reported feeling greatly refreshed.

46

Releasing Performance Anxiety

THE COMPONENTS OF ANXIETY, STRESS, FEAR, AND ANGER
DO NOT EXIST INDEPENDENTLY OF YOU IN THE WORLD,
EVEN THOUGH WE TALK ABOUT THEM AS IF THEY DO.

~ *Wayne Dyer*

Before taking my granddaughter to swimming class, I noticed that my son, Calvin, was not his usual chipper self. His eyes a bit droopy, he told me that he hadn't slept very well the night before. He mentioned that he was planning to take a nap as soon as we left. Tessa, my granddaughter, and I had a great time at the pool. When we got back to their house, Calvin was still asleep.

Tessa, being the rambunctious toddler that she was, immediately woke her daddy up. Calvin prepared lunch for us and Tessa fell asleep in his arms. I asked what was going on, and he replied that he was feeling anxious about an upcoming competition where he was hoping to earn his blue cord in Capoeira, a martial art from Brazil.

I asked Calvin what he was feeling uncomfortable about. He replied that he didn't think he was fast enough. The head teacher at the upcoming event (known as a mastré), had a strong Portuguese accent, which made it difficult for Calvin to understand exactly what he was doing wrong. In the past, the mastré had simply given Calvin a "look" which he didn't understand.

I asked Calvin how he felt when the mastré gave him that intimidating look, and he said, "Confused and embarrassed." He also had a fear that it would happen again – that the teacher would say something that he wouldn't understand and then give him a look that he didn't understand either.

We came up with an Ultimate Truth Statement (which is always stated in the present tense) for Calvin: "I am a great Capoeira teacher. I am proud of my blue belt and my connection to the greater Capoeira world." We had gone over many of his positive attributes and when he repeated his Ultimate Truth Statement, I asked him how true it felt.

With an Ultimate Truth Statement, 10 is the highest. Calvin felt that he was at a 7-8. I asked him if he could discern what was in the way of him experiencing his UTS at a 10. What came up for him was the same fear as before – that he would not understand what the mastré was saying and give Calvin another dirty look.

I asked Calvin if the mastrés' dirty look reminded him of anything. After thinking for a moment, he replied that when he was a little boy, his Grandpa Jim used to give him an intimidating look that was supposed to stop him from doing something wrong. The mastré had given Calvin a similar look.

We tapped on the "power-tripping" glare that Calvin's grandfather used to lay on him. Calvin interpreted that look as his grandfather being disgusted with him. Whatever Calvin's grandfather *meant* to communicate, Calvin *felt* awful. We tapped on the fact that

Grandpa Jim didn't know any better, that he was simply passing on what his father had done to him. After one round of tapping on Grandpa's "look," Calvin laughed. I asked him if he still felt embarrassed and confused about the glare that the head mastré gave him, and he laughed even louder. Calvin got the connection and easily released the old charge.

His Ultimate Truth Statement, "I am a great Capoira teacher and proud of my blue belt and connection to the greater Capoira world," went to a 10.

One and a half years later, I asked Calvin if he had experienced any additional issues with the dirty look that the Capoira mastré gave him. He shook his head, declaring that it was no longer an issue, that he didn't have the fear and trepidation he'd had before. He no longer takes any of it personally.

47

Sneezing Fit Snuffed

OF ONE THING I AM CERTAIN; THE BODY IS NOT THE
MEASURE OF HEALING — PEACE IS THE MEASURE.
~ *George Melton*

My husband sometimes has sneezing fits, as many as 20 in a row! I have recommended that he tap, but he is so busy sneezing, he can't do anything but ride it out. In the spring there is a tremendous amount of pollen in the wind (our windshield is covered anew every day), and he thinks the sneezing is related to the pollen. It could be, as his attacks are strictly seasonal.

This past weekend we visited my mother-in-law. We were getting ready to lie down for bed and Steve started sneezing. One rip-snorting sneeze after another, then another ... well, I think you get the gist. I was about ready to recommend that he use EFT when I realized that he was just too focused on dealing with the sneezing to pay any attention to me. Then I had the bright idea of surrogate tapping for him. I didn't even tell him what I was going to do. Here is what I did.

I started tapping on my karate chop point, saying, (while imagining that I was my husband): "Even though I am having another one of these sneezing fits, I deeply and completely love and accept myself." (Usually I do this three times, but it felt right to do just one, so that is what I did.)

Then I started tapping on my energy meridians …

- IE: I hate this sneezing
- OE: I don't know what is causing it
- UE: I don't know if it is the pollen
- UN: I don't know what the heck is causing it

By the time I got that far, he stopped sneezing. I didn't need to tap any more. If someone is having a problem, and it isn't right for you to physically do anything, you can still tap for them.

Step One: while tapping on your Karate Chop point, say, "Even though I am …" (say their name or refer to them, e.g. that crying baby) and describe what you see. **Step Two:** (still in the first person), "I deeply and completely love and accept myself." Repeat two more times while tapping on the Karate Chop point: "Even though (whatever the problem is, remember to speak in the first person – e.g. I am having a sneezing fit), I deeply and completely love and accept myself."

Then tap on your Energy Meridians, saying a reminder phrase such as, "sneezing fit." Repeat as needed.

48

Mending a Broken Heart

SOME OF US THINK HOLDING ON MAKES US STRONG;
BUT SOMETIMES IT IS LETTING GO.

~ Herman Hesse

"Karen" found out that her husband had been cheating on her with a mutual "friend" for a couple of years. I had worked with her on her sadness during a mini-workshop a couple of months before, and she had gotten her sadness down to a 5/10 before we ran out of time.

We were finally able to connect and have a private EFT session, even though it had been almost six months since she initially found out that "Harry" had been having an affair. Since then she realized that Harry was no longer going to be a part of her life. He moved out, and took all of his possessions with him. He also told Karen that it was over and he wasn't coming back.

When I asked what she wanted to work on, she said, "Sadness." Her intensity level was an 8, where a couple of months ago it had been a 5. She thought it had risen to an 8 because she couldn't see Harry anymore, and a part of her still wanted to. As she put both hands over her heart, she vividly described a heavy, blue, stuck feeling in her chest. The setup phrases we used were: Even though I feel sad that ...

- Harry won't see me any more, I deeply and completely love and accept myself.
- Harry doesn't want to be with me ...
- I allow him to keep hurting me ...

We did a couple rounds of tapping and Karen said she felt more open. We then tapped on, "Even though I can't have Harry ... " and her intensity level dropped to a 5. She said she felt as though there was something pressing behind it all. I asked her what she thought that might be, and she replied that it was the fear of being alone.

I asked her to think of a time, as far back as she could remember, when she felt afraid of being alone. She was surprised to remember when her dad left when she was three or four years old. In thinking about that time, her intensity level of her fear of being alone jumped back up to an 8.

After a couple rounds of tapping about her father leaving and feeling abandoned, she felt a release in her chest that brought her intensity level to a 4. She remembered that she was never truly alone. Two more rounds of tapping brought her intensity to a 2, and she said that she felt more resilient. One more round brought it down to a 0, and she reported feeling much stronger.

We returned to the thought of "I can't have Harry," and checked her intensity level, which went from a 3 to a 2, and then to a 0. Karen said that she felt calm.

I asked if there was something else that she would like to clear, and she said that she was feeling overwhelmed with all of the things that she had to do, and that her intensity level for that was a 9. I asked how she knew, and she said that the back of her jaw felt tightly clenched. During two more rounds of tapping, her intensity went to a 3, then to a 1 and finally to 0. Her jaw no longer felt tense, and she reported that her feeling of being overwhelmed had disappeared.

Then Karen expressed that she was mad at Harry for lying to her for two years. Her intensity level was at a 6 for Harry's lying, and I tried making jokes about his behavior as we tapped and laughed. It took only a couple of rounds of tapping and Karen said that she no longer felt any anger towards Harry, but now felt pity for him. We did some positive affirmations while she tapped:

- I remember to breathe
- I easily find my center
- I remember the Goddess that I am
- I experience the love that is deep within me
- I remember love is always here now

Karen walked away as though a weight had lifted off of her being. She laughed and moved in a way that looked much lighter than when we had started – just one hour before.

49

Relieving the Trauma of an Auto Accident

YOUR PAIN

IS THE BREAKING OF THE SHELL

THAT ENCLOSES YOUR UNDERSTANDING.

~ K. Gibran

My husband and I participated in a three-day workshop, during which we got to know the participants well enough that we missed anyone who wasn't there. On the last day we were startled to hear that "Sandy," had been in a car accident the night before. She had been hit by a drunk driver and was still in the hospital. We were happy to see Sandy return that afternoon at the end of the workshop. I offered her my EFT services.

She called the next day, and we worked by telephone. I had gone to the archives of the World Center for EFT web site and searched for "car accident" beforehand, to get a sense of what other practitioners had done.

I asked Sandy to describe what she saw, heard and felt during the accident. I also asked her to tell me about her fears. I urged her to give the accident a name – like the title of a movie. Next, I asked her about the pain she was having in her neck: the color (red); shape (triangular); texture (striated muscle); sound (ahhh-screaming); temperature (hot); and a subjective rating in terms of the pain (7).

I bundled together all of the aspects of the car accident and Sandy titled it, "Sucks!" So, I asked her to tap on her karate chop point while she said her setup phrases: Even though …

- I was in a sucky car accident, I deeply and completely love and accept myself.
- I was really scared by being in this sucky car accident …

Then we did one round of tapping through the different points, repeating, "Sucky car accident." The next couple of rounds she repeated the following phrases while tapping on each point:

- I was driving through the intersection
- I heard the tires squealing and thought that was not a good noise
- I saw the teal blur coming at me
- I first thought nothing would happen
- I felt the impact of the car hitting the back left wheel
- I was hit and the car began spinning
- I smelled the airbag going off
- It smelled like gunpowder
- I heard the sound of braking glass
- I heard the sound of the impact
- The squealing tires and the impact felt like a smack across the face
- The car spun around 180 degrees
- My glasses got knocked off

- My vision was blurry
- I saw him drive off
- I heard my neighbors talking
- I was pissed that he drove off

Tapping brought her intensity level down from a 7 to a 3 for the trauma of the car accident. I then asked her about the pain in her neck, which dropped from a 7 to a 5 (without directly working on her neck). That ended up being my approach, to tap on trauma from the accident, and when the intensity level dropped for that, I checked to see how the pain in her neck was doing. The pain dropped right along with the reduction in the intensity of the trauma.

We continued tapping for the trauma of the "sucky" car accident. Her intensity level went to a 2 and then all the way to 0. However, the pain in her neck only dropped to a 4. I asked Sandy to look inside and see if there was anything she had overlooked. She realized that she was feeling angry and embarrassed. We tapped on those feelings for a couple of rounds, but her intensity level remained the same.

I asked if there was anything else that she was feeling, and she reported some guilt about the accident, even though it wasn't her fault. I tried using humor, and had her yell loudly about how guilty she felt for driving the car. At each point, I asked her to yell louder. I think the yelling helped because her intensity level dropped to a 1 for the trauma of the "sucky" accident, and the pain in her neck dropped to a 2.

Next I asked her to tap on her Gamut Point while doing the full 9 Gamut Procedure that included rolling her eyes around, humming and counting (I sometimes use this procedure when the intensity level gets down to 1), and it brought her intensity level to a 0 for the trauma, and the pain in her neck was still a 2. Then it took only two more rounds of tapping directly to completely alleviate her neck pain.

During the first 20 minutes of our session, I found out about all aspects of the accident and how she felt about it, and had her describe the pain in her neck. Then we tapped for about 30 minutes, dissolving the trauma of the accident itself. We only spent five minutes directly tapping for the pain in her neck, and in less than one hour, both the trauma of the accident and her neck pain had disappeared.

50

Sunlight from Heaven

THE BODY IS A SELF-HEALING ORGANISM, SO IT'S
REALLY ABOUT CLEARING THINGS OUT OF
THE WAY SO THE BODY CAN HEAL ITSELF.

~ Barbara Brennan

After we heard that our friend Sunlight, a small vibrant woman in her eighties, had fallen and broken her arm, my husband and I visited her in the hospital. The first thing she asked me was, "Are you going to tap me?"

A steady stream of people from our spiritual center came to visit and wish her well. There were seven or eight visitors and not enough places for people to sit. Under those circumstances I didn't feel comfortable doing EFT with her. Then the tide turned, and people started leaving, so I asked her if she still wanted me to tap with her.

She smiled and said "Yes." This was her fourth day in the hospital, and she really wanted to go home ASAP. I discovered that she was harboring doubts about whether she'd actually be able to go home the next day. Her intensity level was only 3/10, and with one round of tapping the doubt dissolved.

As we talked, she started to complain about hospitals and the hugely wasteful way that they did business, pointing to the trash can filled with disposable products (she lives in the country by herself and is a passionate environmentalist). This was the most animated I'd seen her during our visit.

I asked her if she would like to let go of the bad feelings she was holding about the hospital, and she agreed. With her strong disapproval of the way that hospitals did things, she decided her level of intensity was 9/10. I asked her to rub the sore spot on her chest as she repeated something like this three times:

"Even though I strongly disapprove of the way that this hospital wastes things, and I know that I can't do anything about it, I forgive myself for having been upset about this, and I forgive the hospital for the way that they do things."

Then I asked her to tap the top of her head (her crown chakra) with her available hand (she had broken her left arm, and had lain helpless on the floor for several hours before eventually being found by a neighbor) while repeating, "Releasing my disapproval of the way this hospital does things."

As she began tapping on her crown chakra, her energy completely shifted even before she finished the above statement. She was smiling and I could see more light coming out of her face. Then I had her tap on the following points and say:

- IE: Remaining disappointment about the hospital
- SE: Gratitude for the hospital helping me
- UE: Disappointment about the hospital
- UN: Gratitude for the hospital helping me and other people as well

- UL: Disappointment
- CB: Gratitude
- UA: Gratitude

By the time my husband and I left Sunlight's room, the sun had indeed returned to our friend, who is indeed a light unto the world.

Appendix

EFT Glossary

- **9 Gamut Procedure** – If you are a serious EFT student this is good to learn – even though I save it for special occasions. Traditionally, Gary Craig used it between rounds. While tapping continuously on the Gamut point on the hand, the client:

  1) Closes eyes for a second
  2) Opens eyes
  3) Eyes down hard right, while holding head steady (5 o'clock)
  4) Eyes down hard left (7 o'clock)
  5) Roll eyes in clockwise circle
  6) Roll eyes counter clockwise
  7) Hum 5 seconds of a song
  8) Count rapidly from one to five
  9) Hum 5 seconds of the song again

- **Acupoints** – are sensitive points along the body's meridians, discovered thousands of years ago by the Chinese, that can be activated by acupuncture, tapping or massage.

- **Art of EFT** – this is beyond mechanical and rote tapping. By being in the moment, and tuning into intuition, humor, and creativity, EFT becomes a healing art.

- **Aspects** – Gary Craig calls them "issues within issues", they are related to the problem but separate issues. It may appear that EFT isn't working when aspects show up, but they show up to be healed. There can be a layering affect, and as you go deeper, new aspects surface.

- **Borrowing Benefits** – (I like to call it Opening to the One Heart) happens when participants tap along with a group or DVD. Gary Craig realized that participants can sometimes resolve their own issues by tapping along with others, even though their issues may be different.

- **Bundling Baggage** – where you bundle together recurring issues or traumatic events. and collapse them all at once instead of one at a time. Lindsay Kenny is the genius behind this method.

- **Chasing the Pain** – when physical discomforts move from one place in the body to another or there is a change in the intensity or quality of the pain. When the pain moves to another part of the body, know that EFT is working. Just keep "chasing the pain" until you are able to get the intensity to a 1or a 0.

- **Choices Method** – developed by Dr. Patricia Carrington. Normally, I don't use this technique until the intensity level is down to around 3. Then I start incorporating positive statements in the reminder phrases.

- **Core Emotional Issues** – are usually responses to traumatic events. With thorough investigative work, one can help uncover them and brake them down into specific events to be tapped on and released.

- **Intensity Level or Rating** – can be used to measure pain, discomfort, anger, frustration and any other emotional or physical symptom. We use a scale of 0 – 10, with 0 being no discomfort and 10 being the worst we have ever experienced.

The idea is to reduce the Intensity Rating as we do the tapping, but sometimes the intensity doesn't change or goes up. If this happens, we need to identify other aspects, go deeper into the issue or change our approach. Therapists call it Subjective Units of Distress (SUD).

- **Karate Chop Point** – located on the soft fleshy part of the side of the hand between the baby finger and the wrist. If you were doing Karate, this would be the spot on your hand you would use to break a board. You tap on the Karate Chop point while saying the setup phrases. It is intended to deal with psychological reversal. It is an alternative to the EFT Sore or Tender point. See tapping chart.

- **Meridians** – energy or Chi flows through these invisible channels in the body. The ancient Chinese discovered that meridians connect to major organs in the body. The basic premise with EFT, according to Gary Craig, is that the cause of every negative emotion and most physical symptoms is a blockage or disruption in the flow of energy along the meridians.

- **Mechanical EFT** – where you follow the formula of tapping on the karate chop point while saying the setup phrase three times (Even though I have this_____problem, I deeply and completely love and accept myself) followed by three rounds of tapping the EFT points while repeating a Reminder Phrase.

- **Personal Peace Procedure** – a wonderful way to clear toxic emotions from your cellular memory. Make a list of every traumatic event you have ever experienced. Give each a name that describes the event. For example, "Broke my collarbone." The older you are, the longer your list may be. Choose one per day to tap on until you no longer feel any emotional charge.

- **Psychological Reversal** – "When Psychological Reversal is present, it literally blocks progress." ~ Gary Craig. When one part of us wants to change and another part of us is resistant to the change Psychological Reversal (PR) happens. To eliminate PR we tap on the Karate chop point or rub the sore spot while saying the EFT setup phrase three times.

- **Reminder Phrase** – said while tapping on each of the acupoints. It helps you stay focused on the issue at hand.

- **Round** – one complete sequence (see following entry).

- **Sequence** – the order of tapping on the EFT body points (see Tapping Chart on page 165). The EFT sequence that I prefer using is: Inside of Eyebrow (IE), Side of Eye (SE), Under Eye (UE), Under Nose (UN), Under Lip (UL), Collarbone (CB), Under Arm (UA), Liver Point (LP), Wrist Points (WP), and Top of Head (TH). The sequence is used *after* completing the setup procedure.

- **Setup Phrase or Setup** – an opening statement said at the beginning of each EFT treatment which identifies and helps neutralize the problem. Typically, it is repeated three times while tapping on the karate chop point or rubbing on the tender spot and said before doing the EFT sequence. The standard setup phrase is, "Even though I have this _____ I deeply and completely love and accept myself." It can be a really long run-on sentence that is incorrect grammatically, and that is OK. The point is to get to what is underneath the problem – the "thorn."

- **Sore or Tender Spot** – An alternative point to the karate chop point and is used for handling the psychological reversal. The sore spot is also called the "pledge spot" and can be found by placing one's hand as they would for the Pledge of Allegiance. If you use this point, it is better to rub it instead of tapping it. By rubbing it, you help the body disperse lymphatic congestion.

- **Surrogate Tapping or Proxy Tapping** – where you tap on yourself for another person (baby, small children or adults who can't tap for themselves) or animals. The person can be present or far away. You can also use a photograph, picture or line drawing for the person and tap on that.

- **Tailender** – the negative self-talk that sometimes appears after we state a goal or affirmation. It is the "Yes, but …" statement that pops up. To clear a tailender, we need to get to the origin of the negative belief and then use EFT to remove it. Clearing the nagging inner voice – that is what we want to tap on. It takes awareness on our part, a willingness to be still and listen.

EFT ABCs

THE CAUSE OF ALL NEGATIVE EMOTIONS IS A
DISRUPTION IN THE BODY'S ENERGY SYSTEM.
~ *Gary Craig, Founder of EFT*

Every "thing" is created out of pure energy. Scientists have proven
that everything is energy, and that includes our bodies (hence Ein-
stein's famous equation, $e=mc^2$). Acupuncture, which deals with
the energy flowing (or, more often, blocked) in our bodies, is an
ancient healing modality that has been in use for over 5,000 years.

EFT, Emotional Freedom Techniques, is a combination of Acupressure and psychology. Acupressure is a form of the venerable art
of Acupuncture, though with EFT no needles are used. You actually tap on your own body's meridians while focusing on a particular emotional issue you want to release. The purpose of EFT is to
get our energy system back into balance. Gary Craig says that EFT
helps clear disruptions in our energy system.

Gary Craig developed EFT as a do-it-yourself technique and made
it available for thousands of people through his biweekly newsletter and his free EFT manual (since Gary's retirement, these may
not be available). Acupuncture is only performed by skilled practitioners with needles, and mostly used for medical conditions. EFT
can be used for emotional, spiritual, psychological issues as well as
physical problems.

Benefits of EFT include:

- Easy to learn
- Self-administered
- Painless
- Self-soothing mechanism
- Quick relief from painful memories and experiences
- It is portable – you can use it anywhere
- No special equipment needed – just your fingertips

What I am sharing is a simplified, shortened version of EFT. I am including the 9 Gamut Procedure in the Glossary (most of the time I don't use it, though I think it's good to know). If interested in learning the 9 Gamut Procedure in greater detail, please refer to Gary Craig's *The EFT Manual.*

Before you start tapping: Think of a situation that you want to change in your life. Assess the intensity you are feeling about that situation right in this moment, then rate that on a scale of 0-10, with 10 being the highest intensity and 0 no intensity at all. I suggest that you write down the intensity number for later reference.

The Setup Phrase: "Even though (state your specific problem – physical, emotional, etc.) I deeply and completely love and accept myself." Say the setup phrase three times while tapping on the Karate Chop point on the side of the hand. If at first you are unable to say "I love and accept myself," you can tone it down to something like, "I am an OK person," or "I accept myself." See chart on page 165 for the location of Karate Chop point.

Reminder Phrase: This is a short phrase that reminds you of why you are tapping. Say the reminder phrase while tapping on each of the body points approximately seven times.

Example of Using EFT for a Headache

1. Assess the **Intensity Level** of your headache.

2. Tap on the karate chop point on the side of your hand saying one of the following statements three times (personalize it and use your own words), or vary it by repeating each statement once.

   • "Even though I have this headache, I deeply and completely love and accept myself."
   • "Even though it is hard for me to think because of this headache, I deeply and completely love and accept myself."
   • "Even though this headache may be because I didn't get enough sleep last night, I deeply and completely love and accept myself."

3. Doing a round: Tap at least seven times on energy points while saying the reminder phrase – you can repeat the same phrase or change it.

   • Inside of Eyebrow (IE) This headache
   • Side of Eye (SE) This fracking headache
   • Under Eye (UE) This headache is a drag
   • Under Nose (UN) I'm so tired of getting headaches
   • Under Lip (UL) This headache is driving me bonkers
   • Collarbone (CB) This headache
   • Under Arm (UA) My aching head
   • Liver Point (LP) This headache

- Wrist Points (WP) It's driving me crazy
- Top of Head (TH) This headache

Many times I do two or three rounds before stopping and re-checking the intensity level, unless I get a sense that the intensity level has already lessened.

4. Reassess the intensity of the headache. If it hasn't come down as much as you want, write down the new number and repeat the process.

This is a simplified version of EFT. See Gary Craig's *EFT Manual* (available on the usual sites), or the *EFTFree Manual: A Free, Comprehensive Guide to Using EFT*. http://www.eftfree.net/get-the-eftfree-manual/ for a more thorough understanding of how to do EFT. I recommend this book for two reasons - it's FREE, and it's a clear, excellent guide.

NOTE: on the previous page I said to tap at least seven times. What I actually teach is to tap *approximately* seven times. Many beginners need a number, and seven is a good number. However, when I tap, it is "around" seven times per point. Sometimes I come up with a lengthy reminder phrase on a single point and have my clients continue tapping until the phrase is complete – even if that means tapping 10-15 times (or longer!) on that one point. Well, I guess it's a right brain kind of thing. You know ... intuition!

After you learn how to tap (and learn how to follow your intuition), you may skip points. That really can drive a person that is just learning EFT bonkers. So, the number seven is just a guideline for beginners. No need to take it too seriously.

How to be in the Miracle Zone

The miracle zone is an attitudinal place where we are open to the possibility of miracles. The opposite of the miracle zone is either a disbelief in miracles per se, or not feeling deserving. If we are receptive to the possibility of miracles *and* we are in a place of looking for the good instead of looking for things that aren't working, I believe that we are guaranteed to experience more miracles in our lives.

It's just common sense that we are more apt to see something when we're looking for it than if we are not. So, if you're looking for good, chances are you are going to see good. If you're looking for problems, guess what? That is most likely what you will see. As I will say repeatedly in *Touched by a Miracle*, we create our experience of reality based on the choices we make. This is equally true whether we are making conscious or unconscious choices.

Optimism is related to being in the miracle zone. A fascinating new study appeared on November 19, 2009 in the New York Times under the headline "Power of Positive Thinking Extends, It Seems, to Aging." This research on aging and optimism was conducted in Oxford, Ohio and involved 660 people age 50 plus. The study looked specifically at attitudes about aging. The results showed significant differences in longevity – as much as 7.5 years longer on average in favor of those with optimistic attitudes about getting older.

Even though you might like to have more miracles in your life, you may have some skepticism or some doubts. You can use EFT to clear away any negative attitudes, thoughts or beliefs about experiencing miracles. How might you get in touch with negative beliefs around the idea of miracles? Here's one way: write down "I am in the miracle zone." Say it as you write it. Notice your thoughts, especially negative ones, and write them down as well. These will become your setup phrases for the following exercise.

Using EFT for Releasing Negative Beliefs about Miracles

1. On a scale of 1-10, assess the Intensity level of your negative beliefs around miracles.

2. Tap on your karate chop point on the side of your hand saying the following statements (personalize it and use your own words). Say statement 3 times.
   "Even though I would have to be stupid to believe in miracles, I deeply and completely love and accept myself."

3. Tap around seven times on the energy points while saying a "Reminder Phrase" – you can repeat the same phrase or change it.

- Inside of Eyebrow (IE): This belief that I don't deserve miracles
- Side of Eye (SE): There is a part of me that feels as though I'm not good enough
- Under Eye (UE): I have been disappointed in the past
- Under Nose (UN): I don't want to feel disappointed, so why bother?
- Under Lip (UL): There aren't enough miracles to go around
- Collarbone (CB): It's not fair that I haven't had many miracles in my life

- Under Arm (UA): It's hard for me to believe in miracles
- Liver Point (LP): I wouldn't mind being in the miracle zone
- Wrist Points (WP): I'm not quite sure if I'm ready for a miracle
- Top of Head (TH): It's a miracle that I'm even considering the possibility of miracles in my life

The above sequence is called a round. I often do two or three rounds before stopping and checking the Intensity Level, unless I feel as though the intensity level has drastically dissipated. Next, reassess the intensity of your resistance to experiencing miracles. If the intensity level hasn't gone down, write down the number and repeat the process until you're satisfied with the results.

EFT Tapping Charts

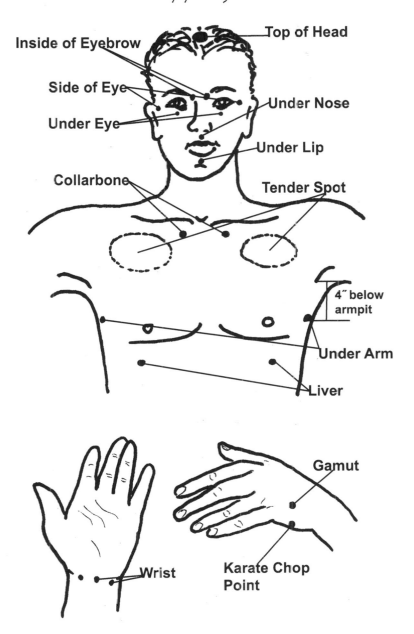

Additional Resources

Bruner, Pamela and Bullough, John. *EFT and Beyond: Cutting Edge Techniques for Personal Transformation.* Energy Publications Ltd., 2009.

Chopra, Deepak, MD. *Quantum Healing: Exploring the Frontiers of Mind/Body Medicine.* Bantam Books, 1990.

Church, Dawson, Ph.D. *The Genie in Your Genes.* Elite Books, 2007.

Craig, Gary. *The EFT Manual.* Energy Psychology Press. 2008.

Dossey, Larry, MD. *Space, Time and Medicine.* New Science Library, 1982.

Eden, Donna; Feinstein, David; and Myss, Caroline. *Energy Medicine.* Tarcher, 1999.

Feinstein, David; Eden, Donna; Craig, Gary; and Bowen, Mike. *The Promise of Energy Psychology: Revolutionary Tools for Dramatic Personal Change.* The Penguin Group, 2005.

Ford, Debbie. *The Secret of the Shadow: Owning Your Whole Story.* HarperSanFrancisco, 2002.

Goleman, Daniel. *Emotional Intelligence.* Bantam Books, 1995.

Gordon, Marilyn, *Extraordinary Healing: Transforming Your Consciousness, Your Energy System, and Your Life.* WiseWord Publishing, Inc., 2000.

Hay, Louise L. *You Can Heal Your Life*. Hay House, 1987.

Hicks, Esther and Jerry (The Teachings of Abraham). *The Astonishing Power of Emotions: Let Your Feelings Be Your Guide.* Hay House, Inc., 2007.

Holmes, Ernest. *Living the Science of Mind*. Science of Mind Communications, 1984.

Jampolsky, Gerald G. *Love is Letting Go of Fear.* Celestial Arts, 1979.

Lipton, Bruce H. *The Biology of Belief: Unleashing the Power of Consciousness, Matter, and Miracles.* Hay House, 2008.

Look, Carol. *Attracting Abundance with EFT.* Crown Media and Printing, Inc., 2008.

Moyers, Bill. *Healing and the Mind.* Double Day, 1993.

Rosenberg, Marshall B. *Non-Violent Communication: A Language of Life.* PuddleDancer Press, 1999.

Ryals, Steve. *Drunk with Wonder: Awakening to the God Within.* Rock Creek Press, 2006.

Shapiro, Debbie. *Healing Mind, Healing Body.* Collins and Brown, 2007.

Siegel, Bernie S., MD. *Love, Medicine & Miracles.* Harper and Row, 1986.

Zacharias-Miller, Carna; Shaner, Lynne; Barbee, Jade; and Morre-Hafter, Betty. *The EFTfree Manual: A Free, Comprehensive Guide to Using EFT.* http://www.eftfree.net/get-the-eftfree-manual/, 2010.

Feelings when Needs are not Fulfilled

Abandoned	Discarded	Imperfect	Restricted
Abhorred	Discontented	Inadequate	Rundown
Abused	Discouraged	Incapable	Sadness
Accused	Disgraced	Incensed	Scared
Afraid	Disgusted	Incomplete	Scorned
Aggressive	Disheartened	Infuriated	Shaken
Agitated	Dishonored	Insecure	Shame
Alarmed	Dismal	In shock	Shamed
Angry	Dismayed	Insulted	Shocked
Anguish	Distraught	Intimidated	Snowed-under
Angst	Distressed	Inundated	Snubbed
Annoyed	Disturbed	Irate	Sorrow
Apprehensive	Doubted	Irritated	Sorry for Yourself
Ashamed	Down	Isolated	Startled
At Fault	Downhearted	Let Down	Stressed
Attacked	Edgy	Limited	Struggling
Anxious	Embarrassed	Longing	Tense
Betrayed	Empty	Low	Terrified
Bitter	Enraged	Mad	Tested
Blame	Exposed	Melancholic	Threatened
Bothered	Fearful	Miserable	Tormented
Burdened	Fed-up	Misjudged	Trapped
Cast-off	Flat	Mistreated	Troubled
Chaotic	Foolish	Misunderstood	Turmoil
Cheated	Forced	Negative	Unbalanced
Conflict	Forlorn	Neglected	Uncomfortable
Concerned	Forsaken	Nervous	Under-pressure
Confused	Frightened	Obliged	Underprivileged
Constrained	Fuming	Offended	Uneasy
Contempt	Furious	On-edge	Unhappy
Compelled	At Fault	Oppressed	Unloved
Criticized	Gloomy	Outraged	Unprotected
Deceived	Grief-stricken	Overwhelmed	Unsupported
Defective	Guilt-ridden	Panicky	Unwanted
Defenseless	Guilty	Panic-stricken	Upheaval
Defensive	Harassed	Pessimistic	Upset
Dejected	Hassled	Petrified	Uptight
Demoralized	Hated	Pissed off	Used
Depressed	Hatred	Plagued	Useless
Deprived	Heartache	Rage	Violated
Deserted	Heavy	Regret	Vulnerable
Despair	Helpless	Rejected	Weighed-down
Desperate	Hopeless	Refused	Worn
Destitute	Horrified	Remorse	Worn-out
Disadvantaged	Humiliated	Resentful	Worried
Disappointed	Hurt	Restless	

Please Stay in Touch ...

Thank you for getting *Touched by a Miracle: EFT Healing Stories*. I hope my stories have inspired you to step out of your comfort zone and, as Gary Craig says, "Try it on everything!"

If you're interested in being part of our community, you can sign up on my website, www.wayhealthy.us. Just click on "Join Free" under Community Options on the upper right of the home page. If you're only interested in my newsletter, you can sign up on the far upper right of my home page, where it says, "Sign up for email feed."

Be sure to take a look at my short *Tap 'n Bitch* video, available on YouTube (just do a search on my name). It is a simple way to learn the points, and something you can use right away. I have a number of other short videos as well, including highlights from three different sessions.

You may be interested in a session with me. If you are in the US, I will cover the phone charges. For current rates, go to my website, www.wayhealthy.us, and click on SERVICES. Or email me at joann@wayhealthy.us or call 707-462-2501. I love working with groups, and am especially fond of what is known as Opening to the One Heart (group EFT).

I really love working with coaches and EFT practitioners! My rates are the same as for personal sessions. If you would like help with set-up phrases, another perspective regarding a client's issues, or would simply like some personal guidance, I'm here to help!

Besides being a Spiritual Coach, I am also a visual artist. The cover photo is one of my most popular. You can get it as a fine art print or card at http://bit.ly/ctfMxK. It is also available on high-quality tee-shirts, mugs and other products, you can get it at http://bit.ly/4Vj9Yh. You can see more of my photo art at http://joann-skywatcher.artistwebsites.com/.

If you want to be inspired on a daily basis, you can follow me on Twitter. I am @MiraclesGoddess.

Also, if you are interested in receiving my husband's FREE *Drunk with Wonder* newsletter, sign up on his home page, www.drunkwithwonder.com.